Maw on Corporate Governance

Nigel Graham Maw
Lord Lane of Horsell
Sir Michael Craig-Cooper CBE TD DL

Edited by
Alison Alsbury

ASHGATE

DARTMOUTH

Published by
Dartmouth Publishing Company
Ashgate Publishing Limited
Gower House
Croft Road
Aldershot
Hants GU11 3HR
England

Ashgate Publishing Company
Suite 420
101 Cherry Street
Burlington, VT 05401-4405
USA

Ashgate website: http://www.ashgate.com

British Library Cataloguing in Publication Data
Maw, Nigel Graham
  Maw on Corporate Governance
  I. Title   II. Alsbury, Alison
  338.74

Library of Congress Cataloging-in-Publication Data
Maw, Nigel Graham.
  Maw on corporate governance / Nigel Graham Maw, Lord Lane of
  Horsell, Sir Michael Craig-Cooper : edited by Alison Alsbury.
     p.   cm.
  ISBN 1-85521-378-8
  1. Corporate governance--Great Britain. I. Lane, Peter, 1925-.
  II. Craig-Cooper, Michael, Sir. III. Alsbury, Alison.
  IV. Title.
  HD2745.M35   1994
  658.4--dc20   93-41372
                                                           CIP

Reprinted 2003

ISBN 1 85521 378 8

Printed in Great Britain by Biddles Limited,
Guildford and King's Lynn.

Contents

Biographies

Nigel Graham Maw

Nigel Graham Maw read Modern Languages and Law at Pembroke College Cambridge and then obtained a Cambridge Master of Laws degree. He joined Rowe & Maw in 1958, becoming a partner in 1961 and senior partner in 1976. He became a consultant to the firm in May 1993. He has, throughout his practising life, specialised in corporate and commercial law with particular emphasis on mergers and acquisitions, often with an international dimension.

He has served as director and also as chairman of a number of companies, including fully listed plcs.

In addition he lectures widely, in the UK and abroad, on corporate matters, and has been a regular speaker for the Institute of Directors at their courses on the Company Director. His firm has published two books he has written on "UK Public Company Takeovers and Mergers" and on "The Legal Aspects of the Role of the Company Director".

On 1 October 1992, he took up appointment as a part time Special Professor of Law at Nottingham University.

Lord Lane of Horsell

Peter Lane qualified as a chartered accountant in 1948 following service in the RNVR and was in public practice until he retired on 30 April 1992, having then been senior partner of BDO Binder Hamlyn since 1979. He serves as chairman or as a non-executive director of a number of public companies and is also chairman of two national charities.

He was knighted in 1984 and given a life peerage in the 1990 Queen's Birthday Honours.

Sir Michael Craig-Cooper CBE TD DL

Michael Craig-Cooper is associated with Korn/Ferry Carré/Orban International, one of the largest international firms of consultants specialising in executive search, human resource management, management audit and other human resource consultancy activities.

Having completed his National Service, he was articled to the senior partner of Jaques & Company - Sir Arthur Driver, President of the Law Society. He qualified as a solicitor in 1961, and joined Allen & Overy in 1962. He was subsequently invited to join the European subsidiary of the International Nickel Company of Canada Limited ("Inco") in 1964 with which he remained for twenty years serving on Boards in Europe, Asia, the Pacific Territories, the Middle East and the UK.

He joined the field of consultancy in 1984 (whilst remaining a director of certain Inco Companies in Europe, the Middle East and the UK). He also maintained outside interests by serving on the board of a property and investment company as well as the investment panel of a public sector pension fund. He is a Fellow by examination of the Chartered Institute of Arbitrators.

He is the co-author, with Philippe De Backer, of "Management Audit - How to create an effective management team', published by Financial Times/Pitman Publishing.

He was knighted in 1991.

Alison Alsbury

Alison Alsbury read Modern History at St Hilda's College, Oxford. She works mostly as a freelance writer, as well as running a small translation business in the West Midlands. She recently researched and wrote 'European Executive Training: A Handbook for Managers' for Financial Times/Pitman Publishing, and has edited a variety of legal, economic and business books.

Much of her work combines her language and writing skills - another example being editing a report on the harmonisation of European product liability law for an Anglo-German research trust. She also acts as editor for the management consultancy firm, London Economics - and teaches music part-time for fun.

In the early stages this book was edited by Martin Briggs. Sadly, he died suddenly in February 1993: the authors record their deep gratitude for his help and encouragement.

The authors have donated the royalties from the sale of this book to the Winchester Cathedral Trust.

31 August 1993

Foreword

Over recent years company failures, financial difficulties, fraud and other scandals have brought corporate governance to the top of the boardroom agenda. The days when directors were the silent voices are no longer. A chairman needs to ensure he has around him a high calibre, challenging but cohesive group who participate actively, encouraging and enabling them to play their full part in the work of the board. The interests of shareholders, employees and all others who have a stake in the company demand no less.

Responsibility to the stakeholders of a company starts in the boardroom. Both executive and non-executive directors must share responsibility for policy development and implementation. Non-executive directors have an increasing and onerous role both in monitoring a company's performance and its internal controls.

Non-executive directors not only provide a check and balance upon executive management. They also bring additional valuable expertise and a different perspective. This helps companies to focus on the key issues of strategy, performance, resources, succession plans and standards of conduct. The role of corporate governance is not just to preserve the integrity and honesty of a company. It is to contribute to business efficiency and development, and so to lead to profitability.

This book is written with a wealth of knowledge and understanding and provides a practitioner's approach to corporate governance. The authors - Nigel Graham Maw, a solicitor; Lord Lane of Horsell, an accountant; and Sir Michael Craig-Cooper, a management consultant - are all highly-experienced practitioners in their own fields. They offer interesting, thought-provoking ideas as to a code of practice and give an authoritative view of the composition, duties and responsibility of an effective board. I believe this publication serves as an important and comprehensive guide through the corporate governance maze.

ALEXANDER OF WEEDON

Authors' notes

Throughout this book, we refer to directors in the masculine. We do so for the sake, purely, of brevity. There are already some noted and excellent lady directors and certainly there should be many more in the future. Perhaps, in the years to come, women will be so prevalent on the boards of listed companies that a future edition of this book, if there be one, will say, 'Throughout this book, we refer to directors in the feminine'. We are, however, united in our dislike of expressions such as 'chairperson'. It is a happy precedent that, in the House of Commons, 'the Speaker' is who he or she is without any need to change nomenclature.

Again, throughout this book we refer to 'UK law', without acknowledging that there might be differences between the laws of England and Wales and the law of Scotland. We believe such differences are minor only, and hope we will be excused for using this terminological inexactitude. Throughout this book we have, for the sake of brevity, referred to non-executive directors as 'NEDs'.

The views and opinions expressed in this book are those of the three authors. Such views and opinions are not necessarily those of the firms or companies with which they work or have been associated in the past.

Acknowledgements

Ruth Tait of Korn/Ferry Carré/Orban International, who helped with chapter 5.

Philippa James of Rowe & Maw, who helped with chapter 8.

Mike Warner of Richard Ellis and Hugh Devas of Rowe & Maw, who helped with chapter 9.

Steve Tibble of Richard Pollen & Company, who helped with chapter 10.

Roswell B Perkins of Debevoise & Plimpton, New York;
Alan Hyde and Ray Sawyer of Thompson Hine & Flory, Atlanta;
Glen Morrical of Arter & Hadden, Cleveland;
Gary Amato of Pillsbury Madison & Sutro, San Francisco;
Steve Pfeiffer of Fulbright & Jaworski, Washington DC;
Gabriel Armand of Armand Boedels & Associés, Paris;
Francisco Prol and Antonio Prieto of Prol & Asociados, Madrid;
Klaus von Gierke of Luther & Partner, Hamburg;
Justus Voûte and Harry Rek of Buruma Maris Scheer Van Solkema, Rotterdam;
all of whom provided valuable information for chapter 11.

Julian Roskill of Rowe & Maw, for his help with appendix B.

Linda Beacher of Rowe & Maw, for production of camera-ready copy.

Lastly, Sarah Mace, for her patience, encouragement and production of the manuscript.

1 Introduction

Some are born with good corporate governance; others achieve it; others have it thrust upon them.

(after Shakespeare)

Corporate governance is nobody's exclusive preserve: it is a shared responsibility of us all.

per Lord Alexander of Weedon QC

Corporate governance as a topic

Almost every day, when you read your quality newspapers, you will find reference to the subject of corporate governance. Not all journalists know what that subject comprises, but they mention it all the same.

Some commentators take too narrow a view, and say it is the fancy term for the way in which directors and auditors handle their responsibilities towards shareholders. Others use the expression as if it were synonymous with shareholder democracy. Corporate governance is a topic recently conceived, as yet ill-defined, and consequently blurred at the edges.

That corporate governance is now gaining such a high profile is no doubt due to the high level of publicity given to certain recent spectacular company failures, despite the background of most major listed companies being well governed.

There is a growing body of opinion that shareholders can and should expect somewhat more of their elected and chosen company directors than holding an annual general meeting, with necessary business being passed through as quickly as possible.

Neither is it enough simply to comply with the minimum requirements of the law, and leave the company's accounts department and the auditors to sort out the annual accounts. At last a convinced and committed understanding is emerging generally that the shareholders are actually the owners of the business and that the directors are there to run that business for its owners.

That the shareholders are the owners is, of course, stating the plainly obvious. This truism goes to the root of the right approach to corporate governance as a subject, as an objective, as a regime to be followed for the good of shareholders, employees, customers, bankers and indeed for the reputation and standing of our nation and its economy.

We must, here, probe further into the consequences of recognising that truism, and look into and analyse the range of inherent duties and responsibilities, obligations and rightful expectations of all those variously involved with governance. A pattern can thus be built up to contribute to the awareness of the topic, enhance internal systems, practices and behaviour, in this vitally important ingredient in our corporate and national success.

The subject of corporate governance has, over the last year or two, received close scrutiny as a result primarily of the setting up of the 'Cadbury' Committee on 'The Financial Aspects of Corporate Governance'. That Committee published, in May 1992, its draft report (to which we refer throughout this book as 'Draft Cadbury'), invited comments (which had to be submitted by the end of July) then produced its findings in its Report (to which we will refer as 'Final Cadbury') on 1 December 1992.

We discuss Draft Cadbury and Final Cadbury in chapter 12 in some detail. We believe that, whilst the work of the Cadbury Committee has made some generally valuable suggestions, it falls short of laying down clear and mandatory requirements of general applicability. It fails to aim sanctions for non-compliance at the right targets (which we believe should be primarily against defaulting directors themselves rather than against their shareholders). Neither has the Stock Exchange responded to Cadbury's mild exhortations firmly enough to match justifiable expectations. We are not saying that compliance with good corporate governance should start and stop with Stock Exchange listed companies: 'it is a shared responsibility of us all'.

As a consequence, we feel that a valuable opportunity has been missed, and compliance with Cadbury (as far as it goes) will become an inconvenient option which can be disregarded at large by the very boards who most need to mend their corporate ways.

Our objective is, therefore, to advance the debate and the standards of corporate governance with reference to our own concept of what that expression means, and to examine the complex matrix of duties and responsibilities of those to whom we should justifiably look to enhance standards of corporate disciplines and behaviour.

The matrix of duties and responsibilities

Our own definition of corporate governance can best be illustrated with reference to the following matrix

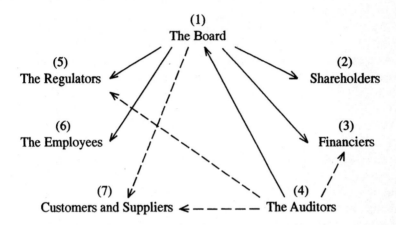

which illustrates the web of interrelationships between (1) the board of directors; (2) the shareholders - particularly institutional investors and the 'City'; (3) the financiers (banks and other lenders); (4) the auditors; (5) the regulators; (6) the employees (as such and as members of the pension scheme); and (7) customers and suppliers.   The unbroken lines indicate the existence of duties and responsibilities existing under general law, the arrows showing to whom these are owed. The broken lines indicate responsibilities which are more implicit in their nature, and thus not generally to be identified as giving rise to legally enforceable obligations, in the absence of a specific agreement, or conduct to the contrary.

Corporate governance encompasses all these complex crossovers of duties and obligations. They are not always reciprocal.

Let us first consider in this matrix the explicit legal responsibilities, moving along the unbroken lines, starting with the board and moving clockwise. The board is the focal point, owing (in their corporate capacity or even personally) explicit legal responsibilities to all the others. The board is owed implicit responsibilities by the auditors in a representative capacity, i.e., to directors as a board on behalf of the general body of shareholders.

Duties of directors to shareholders

It is well established in law that each member of the board owes, individually, and also collectively, duties to the general body of shareholders. These are enforceable against the directors by the company itself (rather than, generally, by the shareholders suing as such).

These individual duties on the part of a director are both positive and negative in their nature and scope. On the positive side are his duties to exercise his powers and functions with proper care and appropriate skill and diligence. On the negative side, a director must not fetter his discretion, he must avoid conflicts of interest (with his own private interests), he must not act in bad faith or contrary to the best interests of the company, and he must not exercise his powers other than for the proper purpose for which those powers can properly be considered to have been given.

The board, acting as a whole, has a further range of duties, namely ensuring that the affairs of the company are conducted diligently, legally and honestly; that the assets of the company are safeguarded and not misspent or misappropriated; that management is efficient and trustworthy; and (last but by no means least in the context of corporate governance) that shareholders are kept informed.

In the last two paragraphs we have summarised, in the briefest possible way, a plethora of case law, legislation and corporate practice that have undergone a process of adaptation, development and change over the years. This process will, we believe, continue into the future, so the job of the company director will become even more demanding and exacting.

The financiers

We discuss the company and its financiers in greater detail in chapter 7. There are, we suggest, certain general policies to be borne in mind by the board and general principles to be followed where relationships and arrangements between a company and its financiers are concerned.

The regular flow of reliable management information to the company's various financiers is vital if the company is to maintain a close and good relationship with them. Reliable regular financial information is important from everybody's point of view - the company itself, the board (for the extra discipline and encouragement it imposes on maintaining the availability of reliable management information to all members of the board), for individual directors (so as to assist them in being satisfied the company continues to have the necessary financing to continue in business, to embark on capital expenditure schemes, to evaluate opportunities for the future of their company), and - last but by no means least - for the auditors, to enable them to be satisfied as to the company's 'going concern' basis for accounting (see, further, chapter 6).

Directors of companies which are going through troubled times must occasionally wonder where their prime duties lie. Do they owe their first duty to shareholders or to financiers? The answer to this dilemma must continue to be found in the basic maxim that directors are there to manage the company on behalf of the **shareholders** generally, and in their collective best interests. It is those considerations which should be uppermost in their minds when considering which type of financing should best be pursued (see further chapter 7). Practicalities and the reality of the state of the company and of its health will however provide a guide to what might be achievable, and choice may be limited.

Duties of the board to the company's auditors, and of the auditors to shareholders

In the matrix illustrated above, we have shown that the board owes duties not only to shareholders (which include duties as to the keeping of proper accounts and presentation of accounts to shareholders each year), but also to the auditors. The auditors for their part are entitled to look to the board to ensure that they are given due access to all relevant information.

As the law currently stands, however, (and we do not see this aspect changing nor do we consider that it should) it is crucial to understand that a company's accounts are its **own** accounts, for which the board has responsibility above all else. Although audited, with an appropriate certificate signed by the auditors on the basis of their work, the accounts are not the primary responsibility of the auditors. In chapter 6 we analyse the duties and responsibilities of auditors in greater detail, and make certain suggestions for strengthening and clarifying their role in the future.

However, increasingly, company boards (particularly the non-executive directors) and outsiders (including the regulators and lenders and trade creditors having dealings with the company) are relying - commercially if not legally - on the accuracy of the accounts, the wording of the audit report and the notes to the accounts, and upon the standing and reputation of the audit firm.

The regulators

We use the term 'the regulators' to encompass a wide range of regulatory bodies, some of which (e.g. the self-regulating organisations set up under the Financial Services Act 1986) are of relevance to certain financial and service sectors only. The Bank of England's regulatory powers are primarily in respect of banks and who can own and run them, and how they should do so. There are also various 'quangos' dealing with certain specific areas - OFTEL, for telecommunications, OFWAT, for water companies, the Broadcasting Commission, and so on. It is beyond the scope of our subject to discuss how each regulator acts upon its own designated area of responsibility, or to analyse the specific rules and regulations of each.

But there is no doubt, from a corporate governance point of view, that duties are owed (by the company concerned acting through its board) to the relevant specific regulators, and they therefore fit into our matrix for general consideration as to duties and obligations.

Of more general applicability as regulators in the United Kingdom, are the Stock Exchange, the Panel on Takeovers and Mergers (for public limited company acquisitions and mergers), the Office of Fair Trading and the Monopolies and Mergers Commission, and the Inland Revenue and HM Customs and Excise - particularly in the realm of value added tax.

Looking out from the UK, we also have (in anti-trust/cartel matters) the EC Commission (for European mergers) and (for mergers with an American dimension) The Hart-Scott-Rodino Anti-Trust Improvements Act of 1986 and the Exon-Florio provision of the Trade Act of 1988.

The scope and relevance of these regulators are huge, and the extent to which they have teeth varies widely. It is thankfully almost impossible to conceive that any group, even the largest of conglomerates, will be involved with more than two or three regulators - in addition to the Stock Exchange and the Panel.

It is, however, important to have in place an established system of checks and balances, with the help and support of non-executive directors and the auditors, so as to avoid any grounds for enquiry on the part of any of the relevant regulators. These should also maintain public confidence in a share owning democracy, and avoid incurring the unwelcome, time-consuming and administratively expensive attention of the regulators.

In general, however, we regard it as very much part of any proper regime for corporate governance that close and regular contact and communication with regulators be maintained. The provision to them of timely, accurate, supportable and well researched information is vital. A track record for reliability will be fundamental not only in achieving the specific project in hand and also, more fundamentally, in being allowed to carry on the group's business activities for the benefit of all concerned.

Do shareholders face their responsibilities?

We all know that shareholders have the right to vote and to be paid their declared dividends.

Is there a two-way traffic here, so that shareholders themselves have responsibilities to each other, to the corporate health and good governance of the company itself, and to the contribution of that company towards the success and repute of our economy?

Ownership in a publicly listed company will be widely spread amongst hundreds or even hundreds of thousands of shareholders. The greater the number of shareholders, the more remote will seem to be the linkage between ownership and the ultimate rights of control which are theoretically conferred by that ownership.

An individual private shareholder has little clout on his own. For the general body of shareholders to have real impact, to ensure that the company complies with proper principles of corporate governance, institutional shareholders will have to learn to work together. It should be their obligation to do so. Generally, their track record is patchy or poor at best, non-existent at worst. In the field of corporate governance and the potential might of shareholder control, the old maxim of 'united we stand, divided we fall' has particular relevance.

The primary legal weapon of the shareholders/owners of the company is to exercise their voting rights in general meetings. Perhaps the most powerful potential use of this weapon is to control the composition of the board. This weapon can most acceptably be publicly wielded when there is demonstrable cause for discomfort, sometimes highlighted by the press. To carry a meaningful weight of voting clout not only to requisition the meeting but also to get the resolution passed, there has to be a high degree of collaboration between a considerable number of shareholders. This all too seldom happens, even in the most blatant cases.

Clearly, it is the institutional shareholders who are most likely, between them, to be able to muster this degree of clout. However, institutions prefer to try to persuade the board to comply with their wishes. This might be to get a chairman/ chief executive to recruit a successor or to split the functions of chairman and chief executive, to get new non-executive directors appointed to the board, or even to have the auditors changed.

The institutional shareholders must lead the way if anything is usefully to be done to impose upon an unwilling board an improvement in its general standard of corporate governance. The issue must be tackled even if it involves rocking the corporate boat, even if it means potentially prejudicing the investment track record of the institutional fund managers. Some (e.g., Postel) have begun to provide a welcome lead on the notice periods in executives' service contracts and the length of rolling notices.

Resolving this issue is in the public interest, in the national interest, in the interest of the very reputation of our listed companies great and small. With the privileges of institutional shareholding 'clout' and financial reward come obligations. All too often today, privileges are not reciprocated by an active response to the corresponding obligations, and this is true not only in the field of corporate governance.

Corporate governance will continue to evolve. We hope that this book will help to stimulate further discussion towards improvements in observed standards of corporate governance, as an accepted and self-regulated system under the aegis and supervision of the Stock Exchange for listed and prospective listed companies, and with the active encouragement of shareholders in both public and private companies, with the active and independent support and encouragement of audit firms.

The undesirable alternative is the imposition of strict statutory regulation. If standards are not clearly set out and established, and are not visibly improved, if those standards are not adhered to and enforced - against, in the first place, defaulting directors - then imposed and inevitably inflexible regulation with the force of law must follow.

2 Directors' duties: the legal requirements

The law is a complex organism, subject to constant change, and its requirements (established by case law and statute) impacting on corporate governance become ever more exacting. Since these requirements must be the foundation for evaluating even the basic and minimal standards of corporate governance, we urge boards of directors, in pursuing an appropriate and progressive system, to be more open and communicative than the law demands. This chapter, however, seeks to review the principal current legal requirements and how they have evolved in order to provide the base legal framework within which a board of directors operates.

The organs of control and management of a limited company

The contrasting roles and rights of the owners of the company (its shareholders), and the functions of its board of directors, are threads which run through the whole of our study of corporate governance.

Companies are artificial 'persons'. They can live for ever, but are limited in what they can do by the powers they have been given by their shareholders. The 'corporate veil' concept of the company as a distinct legal 'person' in its own right, separate and distinct from its shareholders and even from its directors, and with its own rights and obligations, underlies the entire basis of company law in the UK. It is the exception, rather than the rule, for this corporate veil to be pierced or lifted so that others (e.g., very rarely the shareholders and, increasingly, the directors) can be held personally responsible for what the company itself has done, or failed to do.

So far as shareholders are concerned, this corporate veil protects them and confers upon them the limited liability they enjoy. As we will see, the directors of a company as such do not have the same limited liability or protection.

The rights and functions of the board on the one hand, and of the shareholders in general meeting on the other, are distinct and separate - even if, particularly in the case of smaller or family companies, the personalities who constitute the board and the shareholders are largely the same. Directors who are also shareholders wear two quite distinct hats. As shareholders, they can vote in general meetings as irresponsibly as they see fit provided their exercise of their voting rights does not amount to oppression against other (typically minority) shareholders. As directors, voting at board meetings, they cannot enjoy such freedom.

The general legal position of directors and their duties

There is a total absence of any comprehensive definition of the scope and extent of directors' legal duties under English law. Although there are strict and well defined categories of things directors must **not** do, our courts have consistently shown a marked reluctance to lay down any specific, comprehensive and universally applicable yardstick to measure where the duties of a director start and end. This is not only because no two directors have the same background, training and experience, but also because where cases come before our courts, the judge is required to decide only upon the issues before him in that particular case. It is not part of his function to speculate upon what his verdict might have been if the facts were different, or if the defendant director had behaved differently.

So what roles do our courts expect directors to fulfil? We must tread through a maze of (sometimes conflicting) judicial dicta in order to find the answers.

The most recent statute of general applicability is the Companies Act 1985 ('CA85'), and it is not helpful. The definition section (s741(1)) merely tells us:

> In this Act, 'director' includes any person occupying the position of director, by whatever name called.

but it does not go on to tell us how to identify who such a 'person' is, or what such a 'position' is, although we are (equally unhelpfully) told that:-

> In relation to a company, 'shadow director' means a person in accordance with whose directions or instructions the directors of the company are accustomed to act

but a person does not become a shadow director

> by reason only that the directors act on advice given by him in a professional capacity

so that the company's solicitors, accountants or financial advisers, acting as such, will not thereby become shadow directors.

To establish the legal duties of directors we have primarily, therefore, to look at case law which has typically focused on:-

- duties of skill and care, the breach of which can lead to a negligence action being brought by the company; and
- fiduciary duties (duties to act in good faith) derived historically from the law relating to trustees, where again it will be for the company itself to sue in its name for any breach.

The basic rule from case law was enunciated in 1942 by Greene MR in *Re Smith and Fawcett Limited* when he said that directors are bound to act

> *bona fide* in what they - not what a court may - consider is in the interests of the company - and not for any 'collateral purpose'

In addition, a range of specific statutory duties is imposed under a host of legislation and regulation, including the Stock Exchange's Yellow Book. The Blue Book on the Takeover Code may also have relevance for directors of public companies - whether or not their shares are quoted on the Stock Exchange.

The attitude of both Parliament and the courts towards the way directors should and do behave has certainly become far more demanding over the past 10 years or so, and this trend must be expected to be maintained. The impact of the Company Directors Disqualification Act 1986 ('the Disqualification Act') is already being felt where judges are having to evaluate cases of alleged 'unfitness' to be a director, and in so doing a required level (albeit a low one) of 'fitness' is emerging.

If an analysis is made of English case law and legislation in respect of the nature and scope of directors' duties, it will be seen that those duties can be categorized **positively** - ('What I am here to do') - and **negatively** - ('What I must not do').

Although there is inevitably some crossover between positive and negative aspects, it is helpful to analyse the position under these two subheadings.

The positive aspects

Here we must differentiate between the positive duties of a director as a member of the board and as an individual.

Duties as a member of the board

We summarise these positive duties as requiring each director to ensure, for the benefit of the shareholders of the company as a whole:-
● that the affairs of the company are conducted diligently, legally and honestly;
● that the assets of the company are safeguarded and not misspent or misappropriated;
● that management is efficient and trustworthy; and
● that shareholders are regularly kept informed of the company's financial position, its operations and its strategy.

It is, therefore, each director's duty to participate, and share, in the responsibility of the board as a whole for:-
● the creation, and timely review, of the corporate policy and strategy for the company;
● the monitoring of business performance and progress in the execution of such strategy and the supervision of line management in executing its designated functions and tasks;
● the running of the company's affairs; and
● accountability (variously) to the owners/shareholders, employees, regulators, financiers, customers, suppliers and the outside community.

In fulfilling these duties, the board must ensure that:-
● the company acts within its own powers (as laid down in the Memorandum of Association);
● the board acts in accordance with the powers delegated to the directors (as laid down in the Articles of Association); and
● relevant provisions of legislation (not only the Companies Acts) are complied with.

A company is like a puppet, and the board is its mind and will. The puppet will respond only as a result of appropriate action being taken by the appropriate organ of control: either the shareholders in general meeting, or the directors within their delegated powers and authority.

If the board purports, without the authority of the appropriate organ of control (namely the shareholders), to do an act which is beyond the company's corporate powers, then that act may be totally invalid (known as '*ultra vires* the company').

The board of directors will typically have vested in it wide powers of management, with rights of delegation. It must act within the constraints laid down by legislation, by the company's own Articles of Association, and possibly by other contractual agreements, for example those made with bankers, other financiers, loan stock trustees and/or shareholders (e.g., under joint venture agreements or shareholders agreements).

If the directors purport to authorise the company to do an act which is beyond the powers vested in the board (known as '*ultra vires* the directors'), then the directors can be held personally liable. However, the third party (e.g., a party to a contract with the company) will still be able to hold the company to its bargain unless the third party knew the act was *ultra vires* the directors.

In its custodianship of the affairs of the company, the board is primarily answerable to shareholders. There is also an annual requirement for directors to report to shareholders as to their custodianship at the annual general meeting when the annual accounts, together with the directors' and auditors' reports thereon, are presented.

Duties of each director as an individual

Each director is required to exercise his powers and functions with proper care and appropriate skill and diligence, so as not to cause the company loss by his failure to do so.

The scope and extent of these obligations is somewhat vague, since there are no generally recognised standards of the degree of skill, care or diligence required. The position of a director here contrasts with the standards which have been more fully developed by case law for doctors, accountants, lawyers and other professionals.

A director's obligations of skill, care and diligence are subjectively assessed with reference to his own capabilities and experience. Hence, an experienced director will be required to demonstrate a higher level of skill than one with less experience.

The leading cases in which the standards of skill and care expected of a director have been evaluated by the courts are, now, mostly of some vintage. In the older cases, a director had to have demonstrated 'crass negligence', or to have been 'in a business sense culpable and gross' for him to have been found negligent, and consequently liable in damages for falling short of the standards considered appropriate at the time.

Three important propositions were, however, laid down by Romer J in *Re City Equitable Fire Insurance Company* (1925) namely:-
- a director must exercise the degree of skill which 'may reasonably be expected from a person of his knowledge and experience';
- a director is not bound to give continuous attention to the affairs of his company*; and
- a director may delegate duties to other officials and is, in the absence of grounds for suspicion, justified in trusting those officials to perform such duties honestly.

The degree of skill expected of executive directors was determined by the House of Lords in *Lister v Romford Ice and Cold Storage Co* (1957) to be equivalent to that required of any employee, in that the executive director was held to have warranted his ability to perform his work properly. In the case of non-executive directors ('NEDs') who have relevant qualifications or experience, the degree of skill to be expected is now similar to that of the executive director. In *Dorchester Finance Co Limited and another v Stebbings and others* (1978), Foster J held that two NEDs, one of whom was a chartered accountant and the other of whom had considerable accountancy experience, were both negligent and liable to compensate Dorchester. Neither of those two NEDs was held to be entitled to relief (under what is now s727 CA85 - forgiveness of directors who have acted honestly and reasonably). The facts in *Dorchester* were, admittedly, extremely adverse as is evidenced by the following quotation from the judgment:-

> For a chartered accountant and an experienced accountant to put forward the proposition that a non-executive director has no duties to perform I find quite alarming. It would be an argument which, if put forward by a director with no accounting experience, would involve total disregard of many sections of the Companies Act.
>
> The signing of blank cheques by [the two NEDs] was in my judgment negligent, as it allowed Stebbings [the only executive director] to do as he pleased. Apart from that, they not only failed to exhibit the necessary skill and care in the performance of their duties as directors, but also failed to perform any duty at all as directors of Dorchester. In the Companies Act ... the duties of a director, whether executive or not, are the same.

---

*   This is clearly subject to 'continuous attention' obligations for executive directors under their service agreements or letters of appointment.

Our courts have, however, always been reluctant to interfere with the business judgment of directors, and have been slow to criticise the accuracy of directors' business foresight at the time they made their decision, even with the court's benefit of judicial hindsight when the case is eventually tried. Rather than criticise the making of business judgments as such, what the courts will do is to examine the factual circumstances and the motives with which the directors acted at the time, and decide whether the directors then acted with the skill and care of which they were (individually) capable in the circumstances of the case.

Our courts are also reluctant to waste their time by interfering in the internal management of a company if the matter complained of may be rectified, approved or ratified either by the board, or by a general meeting of shareholders.

Obligation not to fetter discretion

Directors have an obligation not to fetter their own discretion. Thus they cannot validly undertake or agree as to how they will vote at future board meetings, nor can they 'trade' their support for particular proposals (e.g., 'I will support your resolution if you will support mine'). This problem can become particularly manifest when the board has to consider increases in remuneration for directors or improvements to their service agreements - hence the importance of having remuneration committees composed exclusively of NEDs, as discussed in chapters 5 and 12.

A problem can also arise for 'nominee directors' (although that designation is not recognised in law). It would be a clear breach of the non-fettering obligation for anyone to accept a directorship or to act as a director of a company on the basis that, as 'nominee' of another, he will, in practice, act and vote in accordance with the wishes of that other (be it an individual or company, or even the company's 'parent' company). It is no excuse for a director to say that, in doing what he did, he was only acting as a nominee for a third party and doing what that third party wished.

The obligation to avoid conflicts of interest is typically treated by the courts as a positive obligation, but as it has clear negative aspects ('don't place yourself in a conflict situation'), we will deal with the subject under the next subheading.

The negative aspects

Fiduciary duties

The extent of a director's fiduciary (good faith) obligations is far more definitive, specific and strict than the rather loose and vague (positive) skill and care obligations summarised above.

The concept of a director owing fiduciary duties has developed as an extension to directors (by analogy) of the duties owed by trustees to their beneficiaries. This extension is based on the precept that those who hold assets or exercise functions in a representative capacity for the benefit of other people must act in good faith and conscientiously protect the interests of those they represent. Fiduciaries must not profit from their office, and if they do so they will be accountable to their principal (e.g., directors being accountable to the company or trustees being liable to their beneficiaries) for the whole of the profit they make - whether or not such profit is made honestly, and whether or not the profit was made at the company's expense. This precept can clearly lead to particularly harsh results where the director has properly himself contributed to the resultant profit made by the company.

When discussing the positive aspects earlier in this chapter, we differentiated between the global duties and responsibilities of the board of directors as a whole, and those of each director as an individual.

In discussing fiduciary duties, we must look at the position of each director as an individual. A director cannot, in seeking to fulfil his fiduciary duties, hide behind a board resolution which might be in conflict with his fulfilling these duties, and thereby seek to be forgiven for his breach. The position here is dramatically different to that established in other jurisdictions, e.g., in Japan. Rather, he should, as a last resort, consider resigning if he cannot dissuade his colleagues as to the error of their proposals, and, as will be explained further in chapter 4, he should be encouraged - or even required - publicly to explain his reasons for resigning.

In brief, a director's fiduciary duties to the company require him **not** to:-

● place himself in a position where his duties as a director might conflict with his or his family's private interests;

● act in bad faith or contrary to what he honestly believes is in the best interests of the company; or

● exercise the powers conferred upon him as a director otherwise than for the particular ('proper') purpose for which those powers were conferred.

He must **not** exercise such powers for any extraneous purpose, even though he may honestly believe that he is doing so in the best interests of the company.

Behaviour will be tested by commonsense principles. The question will typically be 'Has the director behaved as an honest man of business?'

Conflicts of interest

These can and will arise. The most typical and regular examples occur when the board reviews the remuneration of, or share options for, directors, and when proposals are made relating to directors' service agreements.

Most of the conflict of interest cases which have come before the courts have been blatant instances of directors using their position on the board to make personal gains, and no one should be surprised that the outcome has tended to go against the director (or even former director) concerned, and has extended to penalizing the personal use of company information or business opportunities.

Management buyouts ('MBOs') often create a conflict of interest. The MBO team will obviously have access to inside confidential information, and also may be benefiting from an opportunity acquired or personally seized upon by members of the MBO team as directors of the company. As a result, such directors will be subjected to a much higher standard of fiduciary duty than would apply in an arm's length transaction with unconnected third parties. If the initiative for a buyout comes from management, the financial and commercial advantages for the company to sell to an MBO team must be particularly strong and be clearly demonstrated to shareholders. Furthermore, the requirement of the Articles of Association dealing with conflicts of interest must be particularly strictly complied with (e.g., declarations of interest, not voting on the issue, preferably exemplified by not attending the board discussions on the proposal at all). The position becomes even more difficult if there are offers from third parties in competition with the plans of the MBO team.

Further, on the issue of confidentiality, it will be vital that an independent board formally gives advance approval to the use and disclosure by the MBO team (e.g., to its own financial advisers and backers) of confidential information (e.g., management information as to the company's management accounts, business plans and financial position).

Conflicts also visibly and dramatically arise where the board is faced with a hostile takeover bid for the company's share capital, and the directors (or some of them) fear they might lose their jobs if the takeover is successful. The director must not prefer his personal interests to those of the company's general body of shareholders. If the bid is in the shareholders' interests, but not in the directors' personal interests, the board should support it. If the bid is not in the interests of shareholders, the board should say so, even if the position of the directors would be improved if the bid succeeds.

The 'Proper Purpose' obligation

This is, perhaps, the most difficult to explain and understand. Stated simply, even if the transaction or act which the directors intend to carry out or implement is within the scope of the powers delegated to them, they must not exercise those powers for an improper purpose. Therefore, for example, the board cannot exercise its power to issue new shares to a friendly third party to improve the directors' own positions, or to preserve their own control and to water down the shareholding of a difficult shareholder.

The 'proper purpose' duty is still somewhat unclear and inchoate, but must not be disregarded, for its very imprecision provides the courts with a flexible maxim upon which to hang an adverse decision against actions by directors of which the court disapproves.

Other duties and responsibilities of directors

These are manifold: some arise under common law, others under various statutes.

Under common law

First, if directors are negligent in the way they fulfil their (positive) duties of skill and care, they can be personally liable to the party (i.e. the company itself) which suffers loss or damage as a result.

Secondly, directors may be personally liable in 'tort'* (perhaps 'vicariously'** for what the company's employees do/or fail to do in the course of their

---

*   A 'tort' is a breach of a duty primarily fixed by law, such duty being towards persons generally, and its breach is redressable by an action for unliquidated damages. Examples of 'torts' include negligence, product liability, occupiers' liability, procuring breaches of contract, trespass to the person or to land, fraud, defamation, and nuisance.

** 'Vicarious liability' for the torts of others (typically employees) rests upon the person (typically the employer) where the employee commits a tort during the course of his employment.

employment). The directors of a limited company will not, however, be held liable for the torts of the servants of the company unless those directors ordered or procured the acts to be done. The extent of the personal involvement of the director concerned is crucial if he is to be held personally liable for the torts of company employees.

There is a possibility (perhaps theoretical but certainly worrying) of directors being found guilty of corporate manslaughter. Such a claim failed in the Zeebrugge Ferry disaster case, where the judge directed the jury to return 'not guilty' verdicts because the evidence adduced was insufficient for a finding of criminal culpability for manslaughter against the directors or the company (P&O European Ferries). Incidentally, P&O was only the second company ever to face such charges. A Welsh building company, charged in 1965 with corporate manslaughter following the collapse of a bridge, was also acquitted.

With the much more inquisitorial and determined approach apparently being taken by the Serious Fraud Office, prosecutions for fraud and/or conspiracy are also now likely to increase in number - particularly in cases of share hyping, of misleading information being given to the public by directors (or, if given by the media, even if not adequately countered or corrected by the company) and of share support/financial assistance cases (see generally the *Guinness* case, the *Blue Arrow* prosecution, and *Polly Peck*).

Under statute

These range from failing to comply with the filing requirements under the Companies Acts to the improper provision of financial support given by the company for the purchase of its own shares (s151 CA85), to theft (Theft Acts 1968 and 1978) and to liability under the Health and Safety at Work Act and environmental legislation. The penalties range from a small fine to disqualification and even to imprisonment and very hefty fines (e.g. the *Guinness* case).

The Companies Act 1985

CA85 created (or re-enacted) 202 different criminal offences (some of which now appear in the Insolvency Act 1986).

Broadly, these offences can be regarded as falling into three categories, namely those aimed at:-
- enforcing prohibitions on companies and their directors or other officers from doing certain acts or entering into certain transactions (e.g., the

financing of share acquisitions with financial assistance provided by the
company (s151)), and the provision of loans and other financial
accommodation by companies for their directors and persons connected
with them;

● forcing companies and their directors and officers to comply with the
mandatory requirements of the Act (e.g., that every company shall call an
annual general meeting of shareholders each year and that every company
shall lay copies of its annual accounts and directors' and auditors' reports
before a general meeting of shareholders each year and deliver a copy of
those documents to the Registrar of Companies); and

● penalising companies and their directors and other officers who enter into
transactions or do acts without following the procedures or fulfilling the
conditions required by the Act (e.g., issuing shares for a consideration
other than cash without satisfying the appropriate valuation procedures,
and the buyback by the company of its own shares other than in accordance
with the Act).

In addition, there are requirements to be satisfied in connection with issuing
new shares, prospectuses, the contents of annual accounts and reports, and so on.
The Financial Services Act 1986 ('FSA') is a veritable minefield of further (new
or amending) provisions relevant to issuing new securities, takeover offers and
insider dealing.

None of these provisions should, in practice, be a worry to directors of
companies who behave honestly and straightforwardly and who have the benefit
of a skilled and diligent company secretary, reliable auditors, and experienced
legal and financial advisers. If boards of directors fail to consult and heed the
independent advice of those they commission to help them, and if they fail to
provide all those independent advisers with full, complete and honest explanations,
then the directors will have only themselves to blame if things go wrong, and they
will have to be answerable accordingly.

Other areas of potential concern

Further duties are specifically placed on directors by a wide range of statute law.
The Companies Acts impose a number of obligations as we have already seen.
One of the text books on the subject contains a tabular list which is 44 pages long
setting out the various statutory offences (with their corresponding penalties)
which directors might commit. In 1988 some 2,500 company directors appeared
in court on charges relating to non-compliance with these duties, and more than

1,400 were convicted in the year to October 1989. A number of directors have suffered disqualification for such offences.

The Company Securities (Insider Dealing) Act 1985 ('the Insider Dealing Act') is a further area of statutory concern (see chapter 3), as is also the Insolvency Act 1986.

Faced with such a plethora of legislation, the prudent board of directors should consider commissioning from time to time legal and environmental audits of its affairs, so that there is both an increased awareness of the various statutory requirements which might be relevant to the company concerned, and an opportunity to put things right or prevent them going wrong. We discuss some of these matters further in chapter 9.

To whom are the duties of a director owed? Who can enforce them?

The company itself

The clear answer to the questions posed at the heading to this section is that such duties are primarily owed to **the company itself** rather than to its shareholders, creditors or employees.

It is thus for the company itself to sue directors if they are in breach, commencing legal action in the company's own name on the authority of a board resolution or of an ordinary resolution (passed by the shareholders). It is not for individual shareholders or a group of shareholders to issue the writ in their names, as a class. Class actions as such are not available in our courts (although they are in America where they are widely and frequently used, as they also are in some other jurisdictions).

This requirement, namely that it is for the company to sue in its name on the authority of such a resolution, presents obvious procedural difficulties to shareholders who believe a director (or, even worse, all the directors) have breached their obligations to the company, but where the board will do nothing about it - perhaps out of motives of self-preservation. What therefore is their position?

The position of shareholders generally: what can they do?

Is a shareholder precluded from seeking redress for the company if the board steadfastly refuses to authorise proceedings being brought in the company's name against a delinquent director where he cannot obtain sufficient support from other shareholders to get the requisite ordinary resolution passed?

The answer is 'No': such a shareholder is **not** totally so precluded, but it must be said that the odds are so heavily stacked against him as to make his chances of legal redress if not virtually non-existent, then certainly difficult and very expensive.

There are, however, two theoretical possibilities open to him:-

- an application by a shareholder under s459 CA85 'on the ground that the company's affairs are being or have been conducted in a manner which is **unfairly prejudicial to the interests of its members generally or of some part of its members** (including at least himself) or that any actual or proposed act or omission of the company ... is or would be so prejudicial'.

  To found such an action on this basis a shareholder would have to argue that 'unfair prejudice' arises because the board 'omitted' to pass the requisite resolution authorising proceedings to be brought; not an easy thing to prove.

  Furthermore, if the shareholders validly ratify by ordinary resolution what a director, in breach of his obligations, has done then that would be an end of the matter, and no remedy would be available.

- A derivative action brought by a shareholder in his own name for the company's benefit (joining the company as party to the proceedings). But such an action is **only** available in cases involving:-
    - acts which are *ultra vires* the company (now unusual in view of CA89);
    - acts which are illegal;
    - acts which are in breach of the company's Memorandum or Articles of Association;
    - fraud;
    - oppression of minority shareholders (thus perhaps overlapping the basis for a s459 action); or
    - breaches of fiduciary duties by directors.

Employees? What can they do?

There is now a positive (but somewhat ephemeral) duty owed to employees under s309(1) CA85. Directors must, the subsection says, have regard to the 'interests of **the company's employees in general** as well as the interests of its members'. But this requirement is extremely vague and can be manifestly impracticable and indeed unrealistic as it seeks to reconcile what can often be demonstrably conflicting interests.

It seems that minimal 'regard' to employees' interests will suffice to comply with s309, for example: 'We, the board, have thought about the interests of employees in some depth but, sorry, there is nothing we can do to help.' Anyway, neither employees (nor trade unions on their behalf) can take court action against the directors to enforce this obligation, nor can they claim damages for its breach or compel the company to take employees' interests into account, and this applies even to an employee who is also a shareholder, because he would be seeking to enforce his employee interests in that capacity and not by virtue of his being a shareholder. Few good employers would regard minimal attention to employees' interests as adequate.

We discuss Health and Safety for employees in chapter 9, and will therefore say no more here.

The company's creditors? What can they do?

Unless the 'fraudulent trading' or 'wrongful trading' provisions of the Insolvency Act come into play, English law currently stipulates that directors can **only** take creditors' interests into account if those interests coincide with the interests of shareholders - i.e., where there is no conflict of interest between creditors and shareholders; otherwise the interests of shareholders must prevail. However, where there is found to be such a conflict in practice, insolvency problems will not be far away and, as a result, there will be a total and dramatic shift in prevailing interests from shareholders to creditors to the extent of the company having perhaps to cease trading.

The public? What can they do?

Directors **can** generally take the interests of the public into account but only if those interests do not conflict with the interests of shareholders as a whole. Thus charitable and political donations may be made by the company, because supporting such causes can, typically, be said to benefit the interests of shareholders.

However, it is effectively shareholders' money which is being given away, and at an annual general meeting shareholders may say that they would prefer to decide themselves what they should give, rather than for the board to make the decision for them.

Directors may be liable to people who acquire shares and suffer loss as a result of false or misleading statements or omissions from prospectuses or listing particulars published by a company in connection with the issue of new shares to the public. A criminal offence may also be committed.

It has now, however, been established by the Court of Appeal*, that the board of a target company and its advisers in a takeover bid can be liable in damages to the bidder for negligent misstatements in defence documents. In the light of that very important decision, it must follow that the directors of a bidder and its advisers owe a similar duty of care to a target company's shareholders as to what is said in offer documents about the bidder, its finances, prospects and intentions, particularly where the bid is to be satisfied, in whole or in part, by the issue of new securities of the bidder.

Moreover, a criminal offence can (s47 FSA) be committed by:-

> any person who makes a statement, promise or forecast which he knows to be misleading, false or deceptive or dishonestly conceals any material facts or recklessly makes (dishonestly or otherwise) a statement, promise or forecast which is misleading, false or deceptive

if the making of the statement or concealment of facts is for the purpose of inducing another person to enter into (or not to enter into) an 'investment agreement' or to exercise (or refrain from exercising) any rights (e.g. voting rights) conferred by any investment. Likewise, creating a false or misleading impression as to the market in, or the price or value of, any investments can also constitute a criminal offence.

The consequences of a breach by a director of his duties

The consequences of a director failing to do what the law generally requires are daunting indeed, and can potentially include some or all of the following:-

- monetary claims being made by the company against the director for damages or compensation for loss (and the company may also be entitled summarily to dismiss the director if he is an employee);
- transactions between a company and its directors being 'voidable' at the company's election (i.e., it can 'tear up' the contract);
- imprisonment or fines imposed on the director for his own or the company's participation in criminal offences (e.g., theft etc as in the *Guinness* case),

* *Morgan Crucible v Hill Samuel* (1990).

or even perhaps manslaughter (as unsuccessfully alleged in the Zeebrugge Ferry disaster); and
- disqualification (from being a director of any UK company) for up to 15 years (under the Disqualification Act).

However, some exoneration or relief for directors from the financial and/or 'voidability' implications of these consequences can sometimes be derived from:-
- the standard indemnity provisions in (the usual form of) a company's Articles of Association, insofar as they do **not** purport to exempt a director from 'any negligence, breach of duty or breach of trust';
- full disclosure of any potential conflicts of interests followed by (independent) board or shareholder approval or ratification;
- an authorising or ratifying resolution passed by a (fully informed) shareholders' meeting;
- s727 CA85 (which empowers the court to give relief in certain cases) and other statutory exemptions from statutory liabilities to pay compensation; and/or
- specific directors' and officers' ('D&O') insurance cover.

It is vital again to remember that, whereas the veil of incorporation with limited liability confers upon **shareholders** (as such) the privilege of a defined maximum potential liability or loss (i.e. the amount shareholders have paid or owe for the shares they have acquired or agreed to acquire), **directors** can have unlimited liability in certain circumstances, and can even lose their freedom (by being sent to prison).

To achieve exoneration or relief by a director disclosing potential conflicts of interest:-
- the director must have openly and fully disclosed his interest to the board (and this disclosure must be read out at a board meeting) and the Articles need to be worded so as to permit it and the director should not vote on the matter: it is preferable that he does not even attend that part of the meeting; or
- the shareholders approve the transaction (after full disclosure to them) by an ordinary resolution.

However:-
- these exceptions cannot be effective so as to authorise or ratify the misappropriation of the company's property;

- a service agreement with a director which has a duration of or requirement for termination notice by the company of over FIVE years* can only be valid if (prior) shareholders' approval or (subsequent) ratification by ordinary resolution in general meeting (s319 CA85) has been obtained;
- contracts with directors (including shadow directors) and their associates which involve non-cash assets of over £100,000 or 10% of the company's net asset value must **first** be approved by shareholders by ordinary resolution (s320 CA85); and
- loans to and quasi loans (e.g. guarantees) for directors or persons connected with them are generally **prohibited** (s330 CA85).

The Company Directors Disqualification Act 1986

This Act enables the courts to disqualify (for periods from two to fifteen years) persons found 'unfit' to serve as directors.

Although a director being so bad or inadequate as to be dubbed 'unfit' must be seen as a low water mark (which no director worth his salt should see as an appropriate yardstick as to what is required of him), the way this Act is being interpreted by the courts (in our view quite encouragingly) is serving to shed useful light on the standards of skill, diligence and attention now increasingly being required of company directors.

What is 'unfitness'?

Under the Act, there is a distinction to be drawn between 'unfit directors of an insolvent company' (s6) (where the court is **directed** to make a disqualification order) and other instances of unfitness (where the court has a **discretion** as to whether or not to make an order).

Insolvency cases

Under s6, an order will be made if two conditions are satisfied, namely:-
- that the defendant is or has been a director of a company which has at any time become insolvent (whether while he was a director or subsequently); and

---

* We suggest s319 be amended so as to require service agreements of THREE years' duration or more or with a termination notice requirement of more than twelve months to be approved by shareholders. Final Cadbury recommends shareholder approval for service agreements or notice periods of three years or more. See further chapters 4 and 12.

- that his conduct as a director of that company (either taken alone or taken together with his conduct as a director of any other company or companies) 'makes him unfit to be concerned in the management of a company'.

In determining unfitness in insolvency cases, the court is directed to consider the extent of the director's responsibility for the causes of the company becoming insolvent, and for any failure by the company to supply any goods or services which have been paid for, as well as transactions amounting to a preference (paying some creditors and not others) and failures to comply with administrative requirements (such as calling creditors meetings and co-operating in administrations and with liquidators).

Section 6 therefore has the incidental effect of providing strong disincentives to 'company doctors' agreeing to be called in to help ailing companies. Is this really in the interests of businesses and the industrial health of the nation generally?

Other non-insolvency cases

The Act itself does, in s9, give some guidance as to 'Matters for determining unfitness of directors', under which the court is told to 'have regard in particular' to breaches of duty, misuse of company funds, indulging in debt avoidance schemes and failure to comply with administrative obligations under the Companies Acts, particularly the duty to prepare, approve and sign annual accounts, and file them at the Companies Registry in a timely manner.

Further, and wider, tests of 'unfitness' have emerged through the courts which have emphasised the relevance of:-
- breach of commercial morality
- really gross incompetence
- recklessness
- danger to the public if the director were allowed to continue to be involved in the management of companies.

Conclusions as to the 'unfitness' criteria

An analysis of case law arising from the Disqualification Act suggests that, provided a director has due regard for commercial morality (whatever that may mean), is not fraudulent, grossly incompetent or reckless, and is not a (positive) danger to the public, he will not be adjudged 'unfit'. But does that make him **suitable** to serve as a director?

Surely, increasingly more should be required of a director as to his skills, diligence and level of attendance and application to the activities and affairs of the company, but it will remain difficult for an appropriately high objective test of such qualities to be laid down. But a flexible self-regulatory system of good corporate governance, monitored at listed company level by the Stock Exchange and, for other companies, by their shareholders with the active participation and assistance of audit firms could remedy legislative and judicial imprecision as to the due extent of the skills and diligence to be expected.

In this area, as in others, it will be for shareholders to judge whether or not the members of their board come up to their expectations. Whether shareholders will be provided (by the company itself or by the investigative press) with sufficient information, or have the resources, stamina and courage to do so in the future, remains to be seen.

3 Directors as investors, directors as insiders

There is strong support for the concept of directors having a meaningful stake in the company of which they are directors. After all, it must be one of the prime objectives of any board to enhance the value of the company's shares, and the more the board sees its management functions leading to added value for the general body of shareholders, the directors themselves included within that body, the better.

Typically, executive directors will acquire their shareholdings in the company not only by market purchases (if its shares are listed) but also, and more substantially, by their participation in share option or share incentive schemes.

We also strongly support greater openness in making reliable information regularly available to shareholders generally. The board can do so by circular letters to them and/or press releases. Boards should be encouraged to make appropriate relevant financial information available to those (e.g., the company's bankers and underwriters) who provide the company with financing or provide support for share issues, and who will not abuse their confidential access to such information.

What, however, is 'appropriate information' for these purposes? How far are directors inhibited or even precluded by insider dealing laws or regulations from following and implementing those matters which many observers support and encourage?

There must be some inhibitions placed upon share dealings by directors. They should not personally take an unfair advantage of the closer and more detailed information they inevitably have (and should indeed have) about the company, its affairs and prospects. Nor should they, by passing that information on to selected others, enable or facilitate such others in taking unfair advantage.

Inhibitions there already have been; further inhibitions are introduced by the new Criminal Justice Act 1993 (CJA), Part V of which replaced the 1985 Company Securities (Insider Dealing) Act. The new provisions in the CJA have been introduced in order to bring the UK into line with the EC insider dealing directive. Whilst the UK Government is bound by the provisions of this EC Directive, the UK Government has in certain respects gone further than those requirements in the CJA.

In the CJA, the two primary offences of insider dealing are covered in s52. An offence is committed by an individual insider with information who himself

deals in price-affected securities (s52(1)). An individual insider can also commit
an offence if either he encourages another person, which can include a company,
to deal in price-affected securities, knowing or believing that that person would
deal, or, irrespective of any dealing, he discloses the information to another
person otherwise than in the performance of the functions of his employment,
office or profession (s52(2)). The circumstances in which any such dealing takes
place must be on a regulated market, or the person dealing is a professional
intermediary or relies on someone else who is a professional intermediary.

Defences to offences of insider dealing are provided by s53, but for each to be
maintained, the burden of proof is on the defendant to prove the availability of
the relevant defence. The defences, in summary, are:-

● the defendant did not expect his dealing or the dealing by the person he
  encouraged, to result in a profit or avoidance of a loss attributable to the
  information in question being price sensitive; or
● the defendant believed that the information had been sufficiently widely
  disclosed for no one involved in his dealing or the dealing by the person
  he encouraged to be prejudiced by not having the information; or
● the defendant 'would have done what he did even if he had not had the
  information'; or
● the defendant, when he disclosed the information, did not expect 'any
  person to deal because of the disclosure'; or
● the defendant, although he had such an expectation at the time, did not
  expect the dealing to result in a profit or the avoidance of a loss attributable
  to the fact that the information was price sensitive.

Section 56 defines what 'inside information' is: it must relate to particular
securities or to a particular issuer (rather than to securities or issuers generally);
it must be specific or precise; it must not have been made public; and, if it were
made public, it would be likely to have a significant effect on the price of any
securities.

Section 57(1) provides that:-
a person has information as an insider if and only if:-
(a) it is and he knows that it is, inside information; and
(b) he has it, and knows that he has it, from an inside source

Section 57(2) provides that:-
a person has information from an inside source if and only if:-
(a) he has it through:-
      (i)   being a director, employee or shareholder of an issuer of securities;

or

(ii) having access to the information by virtue of his employment, or of his profession; or

(b) the direct or indirect source of his information is a person within (a).

The scope for committing an offence (even inadvertently) is thus broad in terms both of dealings and disclosures covered, and the catchment net of directors, employees, shareholders of the company itself, and those working for third parties e.g. analysts, investment managers, advisers, bankers, and even suppliers and customers. The defences (linked as they are to proving what the defendant expected, believed or would have done anyway) are of their very nature vague and subjective.

During the course of the Criminal Justice Bill going through Parliament, the Treasury indicated that current legitimate practices of, for example, investment analysts and institutional investment managers would in no way be hindered or discouraged. The drafting of the Act, however, does not bear out the Treasury's stated intention. Both the Treasury and the Standing Committee were agreed upon the policies behind the proposed legislation, but disagreed as to the effect of the amendments introduced into the Bill. As uncertainty was been created regarding concepts such as 'significant effect on price' and 'made public', the Government has stated that it is committed to considering issuing guidance on 'made public'.

However this would not have the force of law and it may be unwise to rely too heavily on such guidance. Now the Bill has been enacted, we must wait and see what the courts make of it.

Apart from the present legislation and the proposed new legislation, there are other restraints on 'insider dealing' under the City Code and under the Model Code set out in Section 5 of the Yellow Book. In referring to the City Code, monitored and administered by the Panel on Takeovers and Mergers, we applaud what can be achieved by a self-regulatory system as a tangible example of what could be achieved by self-regulation in the field of corporate governance.

The City Code on Takeovers and Mergers

Under Rule 4 of the City Code on Takeovers and Mergers, persons connected with a company which is the subject of a takeover bid are prohibited from dealing in securities between the time when there is reason to suppose that an approach or an offer is contemplated and the issue of a press announcement, or the termination of the discussions. This applies to persons connected with the company who are privy to the intention to make the offer or are privy to the preliminary negotiations.

The Stock Exchange's Model Code

Listed and USM companies are required by the Stock Exchange to adopt a code for dealings by directors and senior employees in securities of their companies. The intention behind the Model Code is that it will provide a minimum standard or code of behaviour for incorporation or adaptation into a listed company's own house rules.

Whilst every listed company is at liberty to adopt its own Model Code, the requirements of a specially designed Model Code for listed companies must be no less stringent than the Model Code set out in the Stock Exchange's Yellow Book.

That Model Code goes further than the CJA, in that the Code envisages occasions where it would be undesirable for a director to buy or sell the company's securities even though he would not be expressly prohibited by the current statutory provisions. These occasions include:-

● where a director is himself unaware of a price sensitive matter under discussion (perhaps because it has not yet been made known to the board) which is likely ultimately to call for an announcement and where, for his own protection, he should be told not to deal; and

● the periods prior to the regular announcements of the results. There is a specific embargo under the Model Code against directors transacting any dealings in the company's shares during the periods of two months immediately preceding the planned dates for announcement of interim or preliminary final results of the company.

Further, the requirements of the Model Code are also more rigorous than those of the CJA in that they:-

● regulate dealings not only by the spouse or infant children of a director, but also by any company with which he may be 'associated' (which essentially means a company in which he has a 20% or greater interest) or by trusts with which he or they are concerned (i.e., 'connected persons' in the sense used elsewhere in company law); and

● extend to the grant of, or acceptance and the exercise of options over, group securities and dealings in such options.

A code of practice (such as the Model Code) to supplement the legal restraints placed on 'insider dealing' is regarded as necessary because:-

- it is highly desirable that directors and employees of listed companies should hold securities in their own companies and therefore they must sometimes be able to deal;

- directors and employees in certain positions will always be in possession of more price sensitive information than can at any particular time be published; even if they do not have it, they will, in the public view, be thought to have it. Accordingly they must accept that they cannot at all times feel free to deal in securities of the company, even when the statutory provisions would not prohibit them from doing so; and

- it enables companies to establish an agreed procedure which provides protection against uninformed criticism both for the company and for individual directors (or employees). It also protects the market price of the company's securities from false rumour, particularly at times of market sensitivity.

These necessities can be satisfied by simple rules and procedures for communication, as set out in the Model Code, or in specially designed model codes. We set out our own suggested Share Dealings Code in appendix C.

It must be remembered, however, that the adoption of a code, whilst designed to make dealings possible, can never legalize a deal in circumstances where it is prohibited by law. Similarly, compliance with the Code is not a defence in law and it may therefore be necessary to be satisfied that a proposed dealing would not be in contravention of the CJA.

Thus, the CJA, the City Code and the Model Code under the Yellow Book, severely restrict dealings by directors or senior employees in the securities of the company. They likewise, viewed as a whole, restrict both the granting of options to directors or employees and, after those options have been granted, the exercise of or trading in those options. Thus, despite our support for company directors and employees to be shareholders in the company, those directors/employees/ shareholders have to accept that their freedom to deal, whether by purchase or sale, in securities or share options of their company is severely inhibited.

Whilst one can understand the reasons for this, the existing law and the provisions of the City Code and the Yellow Book, could be thought to go far enough, and proposals to extend legal or regulatory inhibitions would consequently go too far.

The role under the Model Code of monitoring dealings or proposed dealings by directors in the securities of their company is an onerous one. It is even the more onerous because any criticisms of such dealings are made in the light of hindsight. An inherent, but probably unavoidable, problem, even under current law and regulations, is that it is often impossible, in advance, to predict the impact on the market price of listed securities of a particular item of potentially price sensitive information, as and when such information is or might be published, and whether alone or with other new information.

Whilst improper dealings and the improper disclosure of information to third parties must rightly remain severely inhibited and penalised, both the newly introduced extensions to the law and even the very need for criminal sanctions as they now exist in the field of insider dealings need to be questioned. As to the latter, would it not suffice for the director/employee who improperly deals to have to account to the company for the whole of the proceeds of the sale or, in the case of a purchase, for the shares bought to be held for the account of the company? It is their fiduciary duty under existing common law to do so anyway.

Whilst there would have to be a degree of accountability (to the Stock Exchange and to shareholders) that such (civil) action is promptly pursued (and a note included in the accounts to that effect and as to the outcome), there seem in general to be manifest advantages of speed, a lower burden of proof (to civil not criminal standards), and damages going in the right direction (i.e., to the company itself) to proceed to deal with insiders who deal through the civil courts, rather than the criminal courts. We concede, however that (a) third parties with insider information who themselves deal or counsel and procure others to deal would probably have to continue be dealt with under the criminal law and (b) our suggestion is unlikely to find favour with the legislature.

However, the statistics as to the number of prosecutions brought and the number of convictions resulting suggest either that the Insider Dealing Act was not a success or that very little insider dealing takes place.

4 The company board

The constituents

Many lay great emphasis, as does Cadbury, on the way the company board should be constituted, emphasising the need or at least the desirability for a strong element of non-executive directors ('NEDs').

Cadbury says that every public company 'should be headed by an effective board' and that 'this means a board made up of a combination of executive directors ... and of outside, non-executive directors'.

Cadbury, however, shies away from reflecting what an effective board 'means' in its Code of Best Practice ('CBP'), saying there merely that (CBP paragraph 1.3) 'The board should include non-executive directors of sufficient calibre and number for their views to carry significant weight in the board's decisions'.

This bold pronouncement is made more stringent and precise in Note 1 to the CBP (the notes are stated not to form part of the CBP) where Cadbury says, rather self-apologetically:-

1. To meet the Committee's recommendations on the composition of subcommittees of the boards, boards will require a minimum of three non-executive directors, one of whom may be the chairman of the company provided he or she is not also its executive head.

Not only is what Cadbury is saying in this note linguistically and semantically obscure, even if read in its most literal sense, it is not clear and strong enough.

We have placed the board at the very pivot of our corporate governance matrix in chapter 1. Cadbury emphasises its importance in paragraph 2.5 where it says:-

> Corporate governance is the system by which companies are directed and controlled. Boards of directors are responsible for the governance of their companies.

The board, and the way it functions, will largely be determined by its composition in the first place.

A minimum of one third of the board should be made up of NEDs. This should be mandatory for listed companies, although with time to comply. This would

35

generally seem to be the right minimum for reasons of overall balance of debate around the board table. This provides the necessary members of board committees. Usually and preferably the chairman should be selected from their numbers.

Public reaction to Draft Cadbury raised the apprehension that the introduction of a substantial body of NEDs onto a (listed) company board would produce, in effect, a two-tier board, with the 'doers' and the 'watchers', and with an undesirable element of looking over the shoulders of the executives by the non-executives.

We consider that such fears should be groundless and indeed none of the authors has in practice found such undesirable elements present round the board tables of which they have been members, or round board tables where they have sat in attendance as advisers.

Final Cadbury is sensitive to such fears by stressing:-

> The emphasis in this report on the control function of non-executive directors is a consequence of our remit and should not in any way detract from the primary and positive contribution which they are expected to make, as equal board members, to the leadership of the company.

These fears, further, show either a misunderstanding of the way the board, as a group, should function, or, at worst, show an apprehension on the part of the executive directors of the way the NEDs will fulfil their role. There must, we believe, be an enhanced and growing recognition by the public (and also by the Courts) that there will be a differential of day by day involvement and extent of detailed knowledge of the group's affairs as between the NEDs and the executive directors. The roles of the two are separate and distinct. However, it is when attending meetings of the board and committees of the board that the practicalities of the roles and responsibilities of each director - executive or non-executive - are and should be the same. The contributions of each director should be complementary to those of the others, whether executive or non-executive, and the out-house experience of the latter should be as much valued as the in-house knowledge of the former.

We do not favour a two-tier board structure, and see no necessity for that structure being, in effect, inherent in having a strong element of non-executives on the board. The concept, for the United Kingdom, of introducing a two-tier board structure found no favour with the Bullock Committee, whose 1977 Report said, rightly, that:-

> the formalism of a two-tier board system cuts right across the flexible tradition of company law within which companies in the United Kingdom have operated hitherto.

In contrasting the unitary system in the UK with the West German system of two-tier boards, this Report observed, with approval, that:-

> United Kingdom law has largely left it to companies to define for themselves the role of their boards in relation to management. This has enabled them to draw up their own rules about where the job of the board ends and the job of management begins. It has meant that the distinction between the functions of supervision and management has remained fluid, responsive to the changing circumstances with the enterprise.

There is no doubt that the executive directors have, and indeed should have, a closer first hand knowledge of the operations of the company, its requirements, the hazards of its business, and the possibilities for business improvement and expansion, than the NEDs can have. That knowledge and those qualities should be complemented by, and not be thought to be in competition with, the perhaps wider and more general experience of companies at large which can be derived from the NEDs.

The company board should continue, therefore, to operate as a unitary board, operating in a united way under firm and composite leadership on the part of the chairman. The chairman is more likely successfully and sensitively to fulfil this role if he, too, is non-executive.

Certainly it is the function of all directors to question, and sometimes even to criticise, the proposals or actions of the executives, but this should be seen as a constructive opportunity, and not an opportunity to be resented by the executives. It should not be seen as splitting board members into 'doers' and 'checkers': checkers they all should be. The role and functions of the non-executives must be understood, respected and even welcomed as bringing 'an independent judgement to bear on issues of strategy, performance, resources, including key appointments, and standards of conduct' (Cadbury 4.11).

The chairman

The chairman's role must be to lead and unite, to initiate development and change, and to act as the company's prime spokesman with shareholders generally, with the main institutional shareholders, the City and the press. He should ensure board meetings are regularly held with full supporting information, be familiar with the range of the group's activities, to assess objectively the performance and calibre of the executives at and immediately below board level, goading, criticising, encouraging them where appropriate. He should be available and accessible, particularly to the executive directors; be a patient and good listener, sensitive to problems actual, contingent or incipient; be objectively forward-looking and imaginative, monitor procedures for the safeguarding of the overall interests of the general body of shareholders, and so on. It is impossible to provide a comprehensive list which will cover everything for every company.

Cadbury admirably summarises the 'crucial' role of the chairman in 4.7 thus:-

> 4.7   ... Chairmen are primarily responsible for the working of the board, its balance of membership subject to board and shareholders approval, for ensuring that all relevant issues are on the agenda, and for ensuring that all directors, executive and non-executive alike, are enabled and encouraged to play their full part in its activities. Chairmen should be able to stand sufficiently back from the day to day running of the business ...

The office of chairman will fall for selection, when a vacancy occurs, either from amongst the body of the present members of the board or from outside. We consider it generally undesirable for the chief executive to be promoted to chairman, even if he does not retain the chief executive functions or title. We consider it more desirable that an outsider be brought in, initially perhaps as deputy chairman, with a view to succeeding to the chair after a short familiarisation process with the business, the people, the finances and the outside advisers, bankers and analysts. Such an outsider may already be one of the NEDs.

As to whether the roles of chairman and chief executive should be combined, the authors strongly agree with Cadbury that in principle they should be separate 'given the importance and particular nature of the chairman's role'. We, too, would stop short of imposing a mandatory requirement that the roles **must** be separately held. This would deprive some companies of that rare being who combines both roles successfully and safely.

The selection process

How therefore should the board members be selected?

So far as the executives are concerned, they should be largely self-selecting through their monitored and shown performance in their executive roles. This is not to say that a good marketing manager (for example) is bound to make a good marketing director or a good main board director; he will have a learning process to go through and in this very process, the observations and contributions of the chairman and the NEDs should be helpful - and be seen as such.

So far as the selection of NEDs is concerned, in the past, non-executives may have been chosen because they are friends of the chairman or of the managing director. Whilst there can be advantages in this (speed of selection, mutual confidence already built up, 'one of us' from day one), provided the qualities are there in the suggested candidate, the old boy network should not be seen as the only or even the main source of recruitment of NEDs.

The task of selecting NEDs is not without its difficulties and these difficulties are shared, from different angles, by both the board itself and by the potential candidates. The existing board will want to be satisfied as to the candidate's experience, track record, calibre and relevant background, as well as assess how far his skills and aptitudes will complement or enlarge those already round the board table, as well as form a view as to his clubability as a colleague.

The management recruitment agencies and businesses, of which there are many of high calibre available in the United Kingdom, have a strong and important role to play in the selection process; although the ultimate decision to make the appointment must be that of the board as a whole, the key coordinating role will typically be masterminded by the chairman assisted by the remuneration or nomination committees. Many such management consultants will tell you that selecting and obtaining board approval for the appointment of an NED is far more difficult than selecting and obtaining approval for an executive director, who, as observed above, should be largely self-selecting through proven and known merit 'in the field'. Those who accept the thesis that NEDs have a key role to play will wish to approach the selection process professionally and with the right team.

The candidate, on the other hand, should have a host of questions in his mind to which he must have satisfactory answers before he accepts appointment. Such questions will range over specific matters as well as his general impressions of his potential colleagues as people.

As to these specifics, there is set out in appendix D, a pre-appointment checklist for directors, which should be adaptable to all companies. Some candidates still seem to be satisfied with the barest of all information packs (the Articles of Association, last year's report and accounts, forward diary for dates of meetings) and are happy to accept appointment on that basis, and 'pick things up as they go along'. Then, perhaps, they find all is not as they had expected, or all is not as it should be, and perhaps that there is no real intention to implement assurances they had been given. As a consequence, they feel constrained to resign if things cannot be put to rights, and there is embarrassment all round.

Terms of appointment of non-executive directors: how should they be remunerated?

There are crucial issues here to be considered and applied: they need little or no elaboration and can therefore readily be recited. We set out in appendix B a suggested proforma letter of appointment for NEDs.

The terms must recognise the independence of function, outlook and approach; that directorships involve onerous commitments in terms of duties accepted and time to be devoted on behalf of the company - number of board and general meetings, operational visits and their frequency, predictable volume of board papers, number and nature of committees to serve on - and so on.

NEDs must be paid properly, but not so much so as to lose their independence. As a guide, they must be paid well enough to reflect their duties and responsibilities, but never to the extent of any NED needing to rely on the fees from any one company in order to be able to afford to live comfortably. Should they find themselves in a position where resignation from the board might be the right and responsible step, the prospect of loss of director's fees should not be an inhibiting factor.

We agree with Cadbury that NEDs should not participate in any share incentive or share option scheme, should not in any respect be remunerated with reference to profits or results (e.g., of a specific transaction or takeover), and should not be members of any of the group's pension schemes. They are unlikely to be eligible for membership anyway.

A company car should not be permanently allocated to an NED. In saying 'permanently' allocated, we distinguish that from proper ad hoc usage on specific group business where the use of a 'pool' car is the sensible and best means of transport. Nothing should militate against the independence of decision of the NED. The loss of a permanently allocated car, if resignation becomes a proper course to consider, may risk clouding the decision.

Each company should fund the premium cost for each director (whether executive or non-executive) of his own directors' and officers' ('D&O') insurance policy.

Some companies provide participation for directors in a D&O policy in the name of the company as group policyholder. We do not regard that as a satisfactory solution because, briefly, (a) no director can predict what, if any, percentage participation in a group policy he will be allocated in the event of a claim, and (b) he risks having to pay income tax on the money paid to him by the insurance company to meet a claim, because the money paid can be considered an emolument.

This is an unacceptable prospect. Before accepting appointment, the candidate should check that a satisfactory D&O policy will be issued to him personally in his own name and maintained at the company's expense. He will have to pay tax on the amount of the premium (because it will be considered as an emolument) but that is better by far than being taxed on claim monies: usually, the director's fee will be increased to cover tax on the premium/emolument.

Shareholder approval

Whilst, under UK law, a new director can be appointed by the board, such appointment requires ratification by the shareholders at the next annual general meeting. Further, the letter of appointment or service agreement of any director retiring by rotation and standing for re-election needs to be available at the meeting for shareholders to read. In chapter 2 it is noted that, under existing UK law, service agreements of five years or more cannot be entered into without shareholder approval, and that the authors (and Cadbury) suggest reducing the length of service agreements requiring shareholder approval. We, further, in chapter 6, advocate full disclosure in annual accounts of each director's remuneration and the basis upon which it is calculated (fixed salary, performance related bonus and so on).

Investor representatives

The question is often raised as to whether main institutional investors in the company should be invited to appoint one of their own executives or a nominee to serve as NEDs on the board.

There should be no hard and fast rule. Investors are sometimes reluctant to have too much insider knowledge as to the progress and prospects of the company concerned and to spare their own executives time to serve as NEDs on boards of companies in which they invest. They are also reluctant to be, or be thought of, as shadow directors. Perhaps the appointment of an investor 'representative' on to the board gets the emphasis wrong: each and every board member, and in particular the board acting as such, is there to represent the general body of shareholders, and not a single shareholder or a single group of shareholders. It is dangerous for it even to appear otherwise.

It may be thought prudent for the views of institutional investors to be borne in mind when considering new board appointments (including NEDs). The ultimate choice remains that of the board.

Committees of the board

Final Cadbury suggests there should be a number of committees: a nomination committee and a remuneration committee (whose functions can usually be usefully combined into one committee) and an audit committee.

We have urged that the remuneration/nomination committee should be composed wholly of NEDs: so does Cadbury, and we are sure that this is the obvious right answer. The chief executive should attend meetings of the committee for discussion of other executive contracts.

We would say the same of the audit committee, namely that it should be composed entirely of NEDs, but with the power (indeed the duty) to invite certain executives, for example the managing director and the finance director, to attend their meetings from time to time by prior invitation. The PRO NED booklet on audit committees recently published rightly observes, in the introduction, that:-

> The contribution of an audit committee depends upon the calibre of its membership. This emphasises the importance of an open and thorough selection procedure for the appointment of independent non-executive directors from whose ranks the committee's members should be chosen.

Close links between the audit committee and the auditors are absolutely crucial. Cadbury rightly suggests that part of the duties of that committee should be to ensure the continued independence of the auditors and the availability to the committee of views of the auditors, independent of the views of management, as to the way the company's financial affairs are run.

The board meeting

Cadbury appropriately emphasises (both in Draft Cadbury and in Final Cadbury) the need for board meetings to be carefully prepared. Cadbury recommends (CBP 1.4) that 'the board should have a formal schedule of matters specifically reserved to it for decision to ensure that the direction and control is firmly in its hands'. Most boards will have a formal schedule of matters specifically reserved, and should certainly do so. In large companies, the extent to which the board will have 'direction and control firmly in its hands', will be dependent upon the extent to which the board oversees the work of those to whom management and financial responsibilities have been delegated.

Our Code of Practice goes further. We say that board papers must be circulated in good time; they should be full and sufficiently detailed to enable directors to study the agenda in advance. All directors should be prepared to come to the meeting not with preconceived notions, but at least with a sufficient acquaintance with the matters to be discussed to be able to make a contribution and to arrive at a conclusion on the various issues for discussion.

It must also follow that board minutes should be circulated promptly in draft after the meeting so that there is an immediate record available to all of what was decided. It is a matter for personal taste how complete board minutes should be.

The basis for the decisions made (including reference to relevant board papers), and what the decisions are, must, invariably, be minuted. If any director wishes to record his dissent with any particular decision, his dissent must be faithfully recorded in those minutes together, if he wishes, with his reasons for dissenting. It is not however necessary to draft a 'blow by blow' set of minutes stating who said what and who replied in what manner as to each and every item discussed at the board meeting.

Thus the board will operate as a team, and directors will have available to them a ready record of what was submitted to the meeting, and what was decided.

The secretary should maintain a file of complete and up to date set of copies of **all** papers presented to board meetings which should be available for directors to inspect.

Trouble in the boardroom

Differences of opinion or approach will inevitably arise from time to time. The chairman has the main responsibility to ensure that these differences do not get out of hand. Whilst an uneasy compromise is seldom the solution he should strive for on an important issue, compromise can be preferable to confrontation where the issue is more of emphasis than principle.

It can, and does, happen that, however hard all strive in the general interests of the company to achieve an amicable and united way forward, resignations become inevitable.

This can be particularly grave for the company's future where the 'resigners' have but recently joined the board to improve its governance and its reputation, but the promises as to future action, without which they would not have joined, are quickly shown to have been hollow. A director resigning should make known his reasons for so doing. Shareholders should be told the truth.

Resignation is not an easy option to be resorted to 'lightly or wantonly'. If this precept is followed, but resignation is still inevitable because of the perceived gravity of the situation, than that very gravity points to greater public openness as to its nature.

5 The board and management

Evaluation of human resources

The newly appointed director, particularly an NED who will not know the people with whom he is to work, will not only need considerable briefing concerning various financial and corporate aspects of the company. He will also need to have access to the records and performance appraisals, to date, of all the executive directors and of senior management below board level. A similar process of evaluation and access will recur if, and when, the company acquires another target business and needs to know what it has acquired in goodwill and personnel terms - particularly in professional or service related acquisitions. He will, or should have been, appraised as to the company's strategy, which will normally have been settled by the board, sometimes with the advice of outside consultants and advisers. He will, however, need to know how that strategy can effectively be implemented by the personnel within the company itself and within the target. A method by which board members can objectively appraise existing internal organisational structure, and the key executives within that structure, is by using management audit.

Management audit

A management audit provides an overview of the quality of a management team and its structure, both in subjective terms, and relative to competitors and to the company's own business strategy. It will concentrate on the key executives in each organisational unit, which could include the parent company, overseas affiliates, subsidiaries or divisions, or one or more functions within such a unit.

An external audit (or diagnosis) can be advantageous when an independent, systematic and objective evaluation is sought, unbiased by pressures or resistance within the company.

A small team of consultants will analyse and evaluate both existing individual skills, attitudes and their fit with company strategy, reporting lines, internal information flow and overall corporate culture and how appropriate they are to, and how they fit in with, the strategic objectives or culture adopted. The focus is towards the future: is the management team in good shape for the challenging tasks, and probably changes, that lie ahead?

Some companies highly experienced in acquisitions have their own established procedures for appraising acquired management. Others have the reputation for tough procedures, involving terminating the service arrangements of many acquired managers, particularly at head office. But all too many acquiring companies accept only brief interviews/impressions, and perhaps CVs, as a basis for appraising the calibre of much of the management of the target.

Admittedly, there is usually little time before an acquisition - and none if it is hostile - for external appraisals of the management team. An independent management appraisal can be conducted more frequently than is often realised - even before an acquisition (but then probably only by desk research) and certainly immediately after. These appraisals will be particularly important on acquisition of a target which has performed inadequately: the typical turnaround situation.

There are five steps in the process of a management audit:-

Step 1:   Problem definition and strategy briefing.

Step 2:   Documentation of current organisation and determination of required skill profiles.

Step 3:   Multiple individual interviews of executives, consolidation of findings.

Step 4:   Global profile - systematic individual, team and internal system evaluation.

Step 5:   Conclusions and recommendations for individual management development.

Whilst most of these steps are self-evident, as in most consulting exercises, it is worth commenting further on Step 4, the 'global profile'. This plots the position of each executive, and therefore of the management team, against two broad criteria - years of experience (often indicated by age) and performance relative to expectation.

First, in order to assess what contribution is expected for each position, its specific challenges and requirements are identified (which are likely to be different after an acquisition).

Then, each executive is evaluated against behavioural descriptors. These are grouped into four families of criteria - initiative, competence, compatibility and judgment.

The management audit will give to the board, particularly the NEDs and the remuneration committee, the following (but by no means the only) information:-

Turnaround situation
● Incompetent executives, dangerous for company's long term survival
● Incompetent executives, more inadequate than dangerous
● Inadequate executives, who could improve if trained or repositioned
● Competent executives, to be used as leverage

Team diagnosis
● Analysis of interactions and power plays
● Ambitions diagnosis
● Feedback on respective perceptions and synergies
● Recommendations on team effectiveness

Organisation assessment
● Executives flow (selection, promotion, rotation)
● Structure, communication patterns
● Innovativeness
● Hidden, informal organigram
● Board's involvement

The benefit of a management audit would be that it could show:-
● the strengths and weaknesses of each executive
● evaluation of each executive and his team within the global picture
● a forward looking perspective
● key issues: strategic, organisational, political
● managerial deficiencies
● discreet feedback through a neutral channel

The word 'audit' implies a somewhat sterile - albeit very necessary - process of checking the finances of a company. The human resources, however, are usually the most important asset in any company (even though they only rate a few lines at the very end of the chairman's report to shareholders).

Executive evaluation

One of the prime and continuing tasks of the board, as a whole, is to evaluate those below board level, not only to feel confident about their reliability to carry out management tasks delegated to them, but also to enable an informed decision to be made as to promotions and replacements.

One of the prime and continuing tasks of the NEDs as a group, and particularly those on the remuneration committee, is to evaluate the executive directors. To those who, again, argue in response that we are hereby creating a split board of the doers and checkers, we would ask who else is in a position independently to conduct such evaluation?

Executive directors: their contracts and length of (contractual) appointments

Remuneration is a crucial issue in human resource management; again, the responsibility lies with the board. This responsibility is usually delegated to the remuneration committee. It follows from what we have said when discussing remuneration committees in chapter 4, that the terms of contract and the terms of remuneration of the executives should be settled by a remuneration committee composed entirely of NEDs. Such a committee must be armed with all the necessary facts and details: these will not only involve the remuneration committee having copies before them of current service agreements and letters of appointment, but also details of each executive director's participation in the company's pension scheme, share option schemes, and the like.

The NEDs, as a result of their wider experience and more objective approach, should be able to ensure that the directors are properly (adequately but not excessively) remunerated, and that there is the right package available to the executive directors to give them a stake in the success of the business as a result of participation in share option and bonus schemes. No two companies are directly comparable. Remuneration committees should, whilst being aware of market forces and the going rate, avoid unfair comparisons - particularly with other companies where members of the committee happen to be executive directors.

Cadbury has recommended (and we agree) that executive directors' service agreements should not be granted for a period exceeding three years without shareholders' approval. This is more limited than under s319 of the CA85 which, currently, requires shareholder approval for any director's service agreement which can only be terminated on notice by the company of five years or more.

The practice has grown, and there is no sign of its abating, of directors being appointed under so-called 'rolling' contracts under which at any time, the director concerned is entitled to a constant period of notice of termination. Within the current law, such a rolling period of notice can indeed be as much as five years (under s319). We would urge that, without shareholders' approval, no rolling contracts should be granted to any executive in any circumstances whatsoever if it requires the company to give more than twelve months' notice. This recommendation, clearly, goes further than Cadbury.

In order to achieve general applicability for these recommendations, amending legislation would be necessary, but such applicability for listed companies could be imposed by the Stock Exchange, perhaps through a Code of Practice becoming a part of their continuing obligations.

Other issues relating to personnel management

To ensure that the company makes the most of its opportunities, the board's concern extends beyond policies relating to financial incentives and appropriate remuneration. It will also seek to provide the right environment for its people to perform effectively and to give of their best.

Most senior managers are not primarily financially motivated. Although it is essential that they consider themselves fairly paid in terms of the market place and their own stature and contribution, most are fundamentally motivated by what psychologists term "intrinsic" considerations - the concern to do a good job for its own sake and to achieve against known concrete and worthwhile objectives. Senior managers must therefore enjoy the conditions, resources and freedom to perform and achieve in their jobs.

As we have seen, it is the board's role to define the company's purpose, to agree the strategies and plans for achieving that purpose and to establish appropriate corporate policies. These will include personnel policies relating, among others, to: recruitment and selection, training and development, performance appraisal and succession planning, redundancy and 'de-hiring'.

Strategy and structure

The board is responsible for approving an organisational structure that is designed effectively to deliver the vision and strategy it has defined. Sometimes these will be based on outside reports from a strategic consultancy. Clearly some reports could become dated by virtue of acquisitions and divestments subsequent to the adoption of the report's recommendations by the board and the directors will wish to ensure that the organisation reflects such changes.

The structure will be supported by a system of job analysis and job descriptions which ensure that each position has a 'real job', with clear objectives and performance expectations, and that responsibility is delegated sufficiently to ensure the ability to deliver on objectives.

Recruitment and selection

The board should also assure itself that appropriate recruitment policies are in place to identify people outside the organisation who could provide the skills and experience required in the future, and also a system of appraisal which ensures that people with appropriate qualities, skills and experience have been placed in the right positions. Management audits prove appropriate in a situation of change, which could include a new chief executive being recruited. Many companies have excellent systems in place for internal assessment, appraisal and positioning of executives; an annual review should be a matter of course.

Performance appraisal and succession planning

The board will also need to ensure that an effective performance appraisal system exists to provide feedback, recognition and reward relating to individual performance. Each individual should be evaluated against clear objectives for the position he occupies, and against comparable performance standards for similar jobs elsewhere in his industry. The outcome should be communicated and used as a basis for identifying future development needs. The appraisal system should be linked to a formal succession system, to ensure that the company's future senior management is planned for strategically. An effective appraisal system will help to diminish the operation of the 'Peter' Principle by ensuring that as few people as possible are promoted above their level of competence. In every company, there will be some. Such an appraisal system will take account not only of track record and past performance, but also evaluate conceptual, strategic, interpersonal, operational and self-management skills (including motivation) and therefore the potential of the individual to succeed in more senior jobs requiring these competences.

No system is absolutely predictive. Mistakes about people will inevitably be made. However the board will want to assure itself that the system operating in the company is sufficiently rigorous to minimise such mistakes.

Training and development

The best organisations attract and retain outstanding people because they offer attractive development opportunities, including opportunities for promotion. This includes formal training and courses, but also extends to the opportunity to learn new skills and aptitudes that will equip them for senior and general management.

The route to the top of most large public companies includes broad functional experience, very early line responsibility and international experience. Many of the best companies therefore intentionally provide their highfliers with experience across sales and marketing, operations, finance and other functions of the business, to give them the breadth required for general management. These companies will intentionally throw promising people into the deep end, for instance, to head up a business unit overseas where they can prove themselves. The importance of international experience for multinational and global companies is increasingly recognised as essential for senior management. Many senior managers also benefit greatly from a mentor who takes an active interest in their progress. If these development experiences are valued, if not required, in getting to the top, and ambitious high performers seek the benefit of them, directors will want to ensure that this potential source of competitive advantage in retaining and developing the best people is not overlooked.

The board should receive a report (preferably in person as well as in writing) from the director of human resources on training and management development. Directors should, at that stage, consider the recommendations in relation to senior managers, and take the decisions which they consider to be appropriate.

The board should create an atmosphere in which employees feel that their contributions are recognised and appreciated. If employees are confident that their efforts are fairly and adequately rewarded, and that ability is suitably compensated, they will be better representatives of the company. Training and development, recruitment and selection, appraisal, remuneration and promotion of senior staff should always concern the board, or the remuneration committee. It is vital to good corporate governance that human resources are developed as fully as the other assets of the company; the board should play an active role in this process.

6 The financial organs of corporate governance

In chapter 1, we briefly referred to the duties of the board to the auditors and of the auditors to shareholders. We also stressed the accountability of directors to shareholders.

In this chapter, we will look at the financial organs of corporate governance. To put what we have to say in context, however, it is necessary first to provide a summary of the legal requirements as to the keeping of accounting records, the responsibilities and roles of directors, the form and contents of the accounts and the roles and responsibilities of the auditors.

The keeping and maintenance of accounting records

The accounting responsibilities of a company are placed on all directors, and there are specific requirements and duties concerning the keeping, maintenance and preservation of accounting records, the preparation of accounts, and the filing of returns at the Companies Registry. Boards of directors should see these responsibilities as a positive means of communication and of providing information about the company, its financial performance, position and prospects, for the benefit not only of shareholders and the City but also for others who deal with the company - employees, suppliers, customers, financiers and so on.

Every company is required to keep accounting records:-
- sufficient to show and explain the company's transactions;
- which are such as to enable the directors to ensure that any accounts prepared by them under CA85 will comply with the requirements of s226 and Schedule 4 (see below) as to their content and form;
- so that the balance sheet shall give a 'true and fair' view of the state of affairs of the company;
- so that the profit and loss account shall give a 'true and fair' view of the profit or loss;
- so that such records shall disclose with reasonable accuracy, **at any time**, the financial position of the company at that time;
- which contain a record of the assets and liabilities of the company, and entries **from day to day** of all monies received and paid out and of the matters in respect of which those payments accrued;

and, where the company's business involves dealing in goods:-

- which include statements of stock held at the end of each financial year, statements of stocktakings from which such statements of stock are prepared and statements of goods sold and purchased (other than in ordinary retail trade) in sufficient detail to enable the goods and the buyers and sellers to be identified.

The accounting records are to be open at all times to inspection by the officers of the company. The rights of a shareholder as such to inspect the accounting records are typically restricted by the company's Articles of Association so that he can look only at the various registers required to be kept under the Companies Acts (e.g., the Register of Members and the Register of Charges). Thus a shareholder is typically precluded from inspecting any accounting records: neither is he entitled to inspect the minute book of proceedings of directors or of committees of the board.

Responsibilities and roles of directors

Directors have a statutory duty to keep and maintain the company's accounting records, to prepare its annual accounts, and to lay before the company in general meeting copies of its accounts and the directors' and auditors' reports in respect of each financial year.

The company's annual accounts have to be approved by the board.

Each and every director is responsible for the accounts and their compliance with the Acts, but he will have a defence if he can say he took all reasonable steps to ensure that the requirements in question were complied with. Liability for failure to keep proper accounting records lies not only with the directors but also with 'every officer of the company who is in default' and an officer 'includes a director, manager or secretary'.

Every officer of a company who is 'in default' is guilty of an offence unless he acted honestly and his default is excusable in the circumstances. Anyone found guilty is liable, on summary conviction, to imprisonment for up to six months, or a fine, or both: on conviction on indictment, he is liable to imprisonment for up to two years, or to a fine, or both. Additionally, the director may, as a result of his 'default', be disqualified from serving as a director of any company for a period of time under the Disqualification Act.

Directors are not, however, bound to examine entries in the company's accounting records: they are entitled to rely on other officers of the company to do so.

Form and contents of the accounts

As to the form and contents of the accounts, the requirements are primarily to be found in s226 and Schedule 4 of CA85 (as amended by CA89) coupled with Statements of Standard Accounting Practice (SSAPs) or Financial Reporting Standards (FRSs) issued by regulatory and professional bodies, and (for listed companies) the Yellow Book.

It is s226 which sets out the 'true and fair view' requirements. Schedule 4 sets out an expanded (by CA89) list of specific statutory requirements as to disclosures, format and accounting principles. It is the current Schedule 4 and new (under CA89) s256 CA85 which give statutory force to, and recognition of, the existence of 'accounting standards' as 'issued by such body or bodies as may be prescribed by regulations' - particularly since such 'bodies' are now eligible to receive grants from the Secretary of State to help them (inter alia) with the issuing of accounting standards, and overseeing and directing the issuing of such standards.

Hence, the notes to financial statements (e.g., to a company's annual accounts) prepared under Schedule 4 must, except for smaller companies, now comply with the following new requirement:-

> 36A.   It shall be stated whether the accounts have been prepared in accordance with applicable accounting standards and particulars of any material departure from those standards and the reasons for it shall be given.

Miss Mary Arden QC (as she then was, now The Honourable Mrs Justice Arden) was instructed by the Accounting Standards Board (ASB) to advise on 'The True and Fair Requirement' and her opinion dated 21 April 1993 has been published by the ASB. In her opinion, the effect of recent changes in the law on the relationship between accounting standards and the 'true and fair requirement' were factors which increased the likelihood 'that the courts will hold that in general compliance with accounting standards is necessary to meet the true and fair requirement'.

Her view was, further, that 'The status of accounting standards in legal proceedings has ... been enhanced by the changes in the standard-setting process since 1989'.

This highly authoritative opinion and its publication are greatly to be welcomed for, previously, it was tempting for a company to adopt strange and sometimes over-optimistic bases of valuation (e.g., of installations of equipment out on rental to customers) and still maintain that the accounts (when read alongside the notes which made the position clear to the reader who studied the small print) showed a 'true and fair view'.

Our welcome has particular force, perhaps, since the meaning of 'a true and fair view' has not been definitively interpreted by the courts. Neither has the meaning of 'going concern basis' for the preparation of annual accounts been judicially defined, although that basis is one of the concepts which underlies the true and fair view requirement, and indeed the very foundation on which assets are valued in the accounts. If there is no reality in the company being able to continue as 'a going concern' for the foreseeable future, then its assets may have to be valued on a basis appropriate for a break-up or liquidation/forced sale. Statement of Standard Accounting Practice 2 'Disclosure of accounting policies' (SSAP2) stipulates that a company is a going concern if it will continue in operation for the foreseeable future.

In response to Final Cadbury, a Working Group was set up by the Hundred Group of Finance Directors and the accountancy profession. In May 1993, the Working Group published draft guidance for directors of listed companies on the subject of 'Going Concern and Financial Reporting' which helpfully sets out (in appendix 2 to the publication) a list (six pages long) of detailed procedures which might help directors determine the appropriateness of the company drawing up its accounts on a going concern basis.

Responsibilities and roles of the auditors

Every company must have independent and appropriately qualified auditors appointed by the company in general meeting.

Auditors may resign, or may be removed by ordinary resolution, and, in either case, they may make representations of reasonable length to the company which they can require be circulated to all shareholders. A firm which, for any reason, has ceased to hold office as auditor is required to deposit at the company's registered office a statement detailing any circumstances connected with its departure which it considers should be brought to the attention of shareholders or creditors. In addition, it is a requirement of professional ethics within the accountancy profession that the proposed new audit firm should, prior to agreeing to take on the audit, ascertain from the previous audit firm whether there are any reasons why it might not be proper or desirable to accept the appointment.

The auditors' remuneration is fixed or authorised by the company in general meeting. Customarily the resolution to reappoint the auditors also authorises the directors to fix the auditors' remuneration: the auditors' remuneration for audit work must be separately shown in the profit and loss account or notes thereto.

The audit report on the annual accounts must be addressed to the members of the company and must state:-

- whether in the auditors' opinion the annual accounts have been properly prepared in accordance with the Acts;
- whether in their opinion a true and fair view is given;
- in the case of an individual balance sheet, of the state of affairs of the company at the end of its financial year;
- in the case of an individual profit and loss account, of the profit or loss of the company for the financial year; and
- in the case of group consolidated accounts, of the state of affairs at the end of the financial year, and the profit and loss for the financial year, of the undertakings included in the consolidation as a whole, so far as concerns the members of the company; and
- whether, after due consideration, they are of the opinion that the information given in the directors' report for the financial year for which the annual accounts are prepared is not consistent with those accounts.

The scope of their audit work must be sufficient to enable the auditors to form an opinion as to:-

- whether proper accounting records have been kept by the company; and
- whether the company's individual accounts are in agreement with the records and returns.

If an accounting standard is not complied with, or if the requirements specified above are not satisfied, the audit report must be suitably qualified.

Auditors have rights to inspect the books and accounts of the company and to require from the officers of the company such information and explanations as they think necessary for the performance of their duties as auditors. They have the right to attend any general meeting of the company, to receive notices thereof, and to be heard at any general meeting on any part of the business which concerns them as auditors.

The duties of auditors, which depend primarily on statute (and cannot be reduced e.g., by the Articles) are:-

- to acquaint themselves with the scope and nature of their duties;
- to carry out their duties as to the auditors' report (see above); and
- to act honestly and with reasonable care and skill.

In this context it is worth repeating the oft quoted extract from the judgment of Lopes J in *Re Kingston Cotton Mill Co* (No.2) [1896]:-

> An auditor is not bound to be a detective, or ... to approach his work ... with a foregone conclusion that there is something wrong. He is a watchdog, but not a bloodhound. He is justified in believing tried servants of the company in whom confidence is placed by the company. He is entitled to assume that they are honest, and to rely on their representations provided he takes reasonable care. If there is anything calculated to excite suspicion he should probe it to the bottom; but in the absence of anything of that kind he is only bound to be reasonably cautious and careful.

Neither as a matter of law nor under their professional guidelines are auditors responsible for the detection or prevention of irregularities or fraud: this responsibility rests with the management in the first place, and with the board. We focus later in this chapter on the question of fraud in greater detail.

Although the auditors' statutory and common law duties are to shareholders alone, it is recognised that third parties may well read a company's accounts and may seek to derive comfort from the wording of the audit report and the professional standing and reputation of the firm which signed it. However, it has now been established that as a general rule, and in the absence of special circumstances, that auditors will not be liable to such third parties: auditors owe a duty of care to the company itself, for the benefit of its shareholders, but not to everyone in the whole wide world who might read and seek to rely on the accounts and the audit report.

An unqualified audit report is not a guarantee of the accuracy of each figure in the company's accounts. It can only be an expression of opinion as to the assets, liabilities, profits or losses as at the date of the balance sheet. Hence, an audit opinion cannot be read as a guarantee of values, for there have to be judgments as to materiality, both line by line and in the aggregate.

The audit and corporate governance

Final Cadbury rightly stresses the importance of the audit function and of the independence of the auditors in paragraph 5.1:-

> The annual audit is one of the cornerstones of corporate governance. Given the separation of ownership from management, the directors are

required to report on their stewardship by means of the annual report and financial statements sent to the shareholders. The audit provides an external and objective check on the way in which the financial statements have been prepared and presented and it is an essential part of the checks and balances required. The question is not whether there should be an audit but how to ensure its objectivity and effectiveness.

In our view, that is well said. Audits are of great value for boards of directors. It is important that all members of a board understand the purpose and meaning of an audit. The audit functions should produce an informed, work supported, documented and carefully considered opinion. The auditors are reporting to the shareholders with their own independent opinion.

The primary responsibility for financial statements lies with the directors and with the management of the company. It is the board which carries responsibility for the preparation of the accounts. The auditors' responsibility is to form an objective, independent, well informed, balanced opinion on the accounts. The board can obtain assistance in discharging its responsibility by delegating some of its work to an audit committee, but ultimate responsibility remains with each and every director. The board has the duty to define how the accounts are presented, and to make sure that the information given is both accurate and complete.

In practice, NEDs have to rely on management to fulfil these responsibilities and duties. NEDs rarely have close knowledge of the day to day financial affairs of the company, but should take every opportunity to meet and get to know those responsible for those financial affairs so as to form an assessment of their reliability, calibre, and integrity. NEDs can, further, make a useful contribution from the financial and business experience they have gleaned elsewhere - by casting a critical and comparative eye over the extent, scope and presentation of the information provided, and how promptly it is provided.

To mislead auditors is a criminal offence under the Acts and the board therefore carries full responsibility for both the completeness and the accuracy of the accounts. Boards and auditors have a common interest in good, properly audited accounts, aiming always for greater clarity and consistency of presentation.

Auditors are independently appointed by the shareholders, report annually to them, and are independent of management. They are thus theoretically not interested in the reported results of the company. However, in practice the directors' recommendations concerning the appointment or reappointment of auditors almost always prevail. Shareholders do not have any direct link with the auditors, or much opportunity to seek their views or reassurances, save through questions put to them (through the chairman) at the annual general meeting. Thus the independence of the appointment and of the audit functions may seem to be more apparent than real.

The majority of companies are well and properly managed by directors who are honest and competent. From the point of view of the auditors, it is much easier to audit a company which is well run. The audit can then proceed efficiently, without surprises and without conflicts arising between the auditors (with their statutory and common law duties) and the financial director and his team.

The auditors are watchdogs, but they are not expected to play detective. They are entitled to assume that the management accounts presented to them are accurate and that those who prepared them are honest. The auditors are therefore only legally liable if they has been negligent in performing their duty. They are not liable for fraudulent accounts, only for the proper performance of the audit (see, further, the section headed 'Fraud' below).

The relationship of the board with the auditors

Audit services

The relationship of the board with the auditors should be one of mutual respect and recognition of their differing, but complementary, tasks. From the board's point of view, the fostering and maintenance of this ideal relationship is almost certainly too important to be left solely to the finance director, although if he and the auditors lack that mutuality of respect and recognition, one of them must probably go. Most boards therefore do or should set up an audit committee and Final Cadbury firmly endorses having such a committee.

The typical relationship between the board and the auditors has undergone a substantial change in the last ten years. Hyperactive markets in the 1980s bred a search for creative accounting practices which broadly took place within a framework of what was allowed because it was not legally improper, with the object of maximising the growth performance of a takeover-led acquisitive company. This objective was assisted by realigning expenditures, write-offs and adjusting the target's prior year (as yet unaudited) results, the better to enhance share prices, either to form the platform for the next acquisition, retrospectively to justify the acquisition, or to adopt an attractive defence against an unwelcome takeover.

In these activities, boards were assisted by their financial advisers and by the auditors. Their advice was devised and moulded within the framework of acceptable accounting standards and practices, which provided perhaps too much variety of scope for presenting facts and figures for fair and meaningful comparisons to be made as between businesses engaged in similar activities, or even sometimes for the true nature and extent of the enlarged group's liabilities and obligations - and even its profitability - to be evaluated properly.

The accounting profession has reacted to the perceived excesses of the 1980s and to the many criticisms of published financial statements and of auditors. These developments have initiated a substantial debate on financial reporting standards.

In 1987, the accounting profession invited Sir Ron Dearing to lead a review of the accounting standard setting process in the UK. His committee's 1988 report 'The Making of Accounting Standards' led to the establishment in 1990 of the Financial Reporting Council (FRC) and its offsprings, the Accounting Standards Board (ASB), the Urgent Issues Task Force (UITF) and the Financial Report Review Panel (FRRP).

The FRC's role is primarily to see that the work on developing and enforcing accounting standards is adequately funded. Whereas under the previous regime it was only accountants who paid for, and were involved in, the standard setting process, the FRC now obtains funding from, inter alia, the Stock Exchange, the Department of Trade and Industry, banks and institutional investors as well as from the accountancy profession itself.

This new regime has certain welcome features. Those responsible for the development of standards, the ASB and the UITF, have more resources available to them. Perhaps more significantly, we now have the FRRP, a body set up to investigate instances (where there appears to be a departure from accounting standards or other requirements) which might lead to the accounts not giving a true and fair view. The decisions taken by the FRRP to date have attracted considerable media attention and interest. Our view is that its presence already acts as a powerful deterrent to companies wishing to adopt unduly aggressive accounting policies.

The accountancy institutes have also responded to criticisms of auditing practitioners. In 1991, the former Auditing Practices Committee, which was substantially made up of auditors, was replaced by the Auditing Practices Board (APB), half of whose members are non-auditors. The APB has, in our opinion, made a relatively slow start. It also continues to attract criticism for still being too close to the accountancy institutes and not sufficiently independent. Perhaps these are only teething problems. We hope that swift action will be taken to meet these criticisms. There remain several 'grey' areas, which are all a reflection of changing markets. Accounting practice is changing fast to find ways of more accurately interpreting and highlighting these grey areas.

Non-tangible assets and liabilities continue to present problems. How do you value a brand, or assess and quantify an environmental liability? Discontinued operations, costs of restructuring and reorganisation and other exceptional and extraordinary items all have to be evaluated and then represented in the accounts - with appropriate discounts or provisions. Accountants rely heavily on accounting standards set by the ASB.

Non-audit services

The Companies Act 1981, implementing the EC Fourth Directive, introduced a legal framework which probably added to, rather than subtracted from, the problem. Constraints on the marketing of accounting activity were removed from auditing firms. This enhanced the ability of the audit firm to attempt to market a variety of services to a client which was primarily an audit client. In theory, this should cause no trouble, but in practice, particularly in periods of recession, there is inevitably a much greater financial risk for the audit firm of it having fee discussions with an audit client which, in an era of intense competition - in itself not to be discouraged - might tempt a board to regard auditing as the service of yet another supplier. Audit firms are in competition with each other for business, but ideally the priority should be to compete on professional reputation and performance.

In February 1992 the Chartered Accountants Joint Ethics Committee (CAJEC) published a 'Revised Guide to Professional Ethics' which states that:-

> The fees from a number of one-off assignments could, if taken together with recurring work, give rise to a problem of undue dependence on an audit client... In circumstances where a member is dependent for his income on the profits of any one office within a practice and the gross income of that office is regularly dependent on one client or group of connected clients for more than 15 per cent of its gross fees ... a partner from another office of the practice should take final responsibility for any report made by the practice on the affairs of that client. (Sections 2.5-2.7)

This is because:-

> The public perception of a member's objectivity is likely to be in jeopardy where the fees for audit and other recurring work paid by one client or group of connected clients exceeds 15 per cent of the gross practice income. (Section 2.2)

The 15% guide has been part of the profession's Ethical Guidance for about 20 years. What is new from 1992 is that it also recommends that:-

> Where the public interest is involved it is particularly important that objectivity is seen to be preserved, and in the case of listed and other public interest companies, the appropriate figure should be 10 per cent of the gross practice income. (Section 2.2)

In October 1991, new regulations* came into force requiring companies to disclose how much is paid to the auditors and their associates for non-auditing services (e.g., management consultancy).

These regulations require a company to disclose within its accounts for financial years beginning on or after 1 October 1991, the aggregate of the remuneration, if any, in respect of work carried out in that year, and during the previous financial year (except for the first year), by the company's auditors and by any person who is an associate of the auditors in that year.

The disclosure of non-audit fees has been sought for some time by shareholder groups, as there has been a belief that accountancy firms have become too dependent upon substantial fees earned for consultancy service provided by accountants to their audit clients. However, we doubt whether the information provided will be meaningful without some explanation as to what the services comprise.

Disclosure of the aggregate amounts paid will not permit meaningful comparison amongst companies unless all professional fees are disclosed with details as to the services used. There are, further, likely to be a number of anomalies where, for example, substantial parts of a group of companies are provided with services by accountancy firms other than the parent company auditor.

Auditing represents a judgment by the auditors of the reliability of information made available by management. It is that independent judgment which is so vital, and which all responsible boards (and, particularly, their audit committees) should recognise, respect and preserve.

---

* Companies Act 1985 (Disclosure of remuneration for non audit work) Regulations 1991. The new regulations do not apply to a company which qualifies as a small or medium sized company by virtue of s247 of the 1985 Act, but they do apply to the majority of listed companies.

Financial reporting and the Cadbury Report

The Cadbury Committee's purpose 'was to review those aspects of corporate governance specifically related to financial reporting and accountability'. It was in this area that the committee made, in our view, the greatest positive and valuable contribution. Hence, we endorse what Final Cadbury had to say under the heading of 'The Financial Aspects of Corporate Governance', narrowly construed.

Audit committees

The Cadbury Code of Best Practice states at 4.3:-

> The board should establish an audit committee of at least three non-executive directors with written terms of reference which deal clearly with its authority and duty.

It goes on to recommend that audit committees should be formally constituted with written terms of reference. The external auditor, head of internal audit and the finance director should normally attend; they should have discussions at least once a year with the auditors without executive board members present: membership of the committee should be disclosed in the annual report.

Final Cadbury set out specimen Terms of Reference for an audit committee for guidance purposes, with separate sections dealing with its constitution, membership, attendance at meetings, frequency of meetings, its authority, its duties and reporting procedures. We consider that this is a useful model to be adapted, if necessary, to suit particular circumstances.

Interestingly, the specimen allocates, as one of the duties of the committee, the review (half yearly and annually) of the going concern assumption (see below).

We support these recommendations and firmly believe that an effective audit committee has a prime role to play in improving corporate governance.

We must in general also support the recommendation that 'other board members should also have the right to attend'. They can, as board members, hardly be formally excluded from meetings of the audit committee, although we believe that other board members should be reticent to attend the early and exploratory meetings of the audit committee, unless specifically asked to be present. The whole board must be involved in some audit committee deliberations anyway, particularly with regard to the annual and half year statements.

Public perception of the relationship between boards and auditors veers from the apathetic to the critical. The establishment of an audit committee, its members and designated functions being listed in the annual accounts, and being available to answer shareholders' questions at the AGM, should enhance the true perspective. We would also commend the value of a meeting between the auditors and the full board, probably at the meeting when the annual accounts are formally approved. This meeting would help to eliminate any 'two-tier' effect of segregation between members of the board who are, or who are not, members of the audit committee.

What should be the attributes and requirements of such a committee? In particular we highlight four elements:-

● The committee, consisting as it should ideally do of NEDs only, should regard itself as interposed between management and the auditors. It should remain independent of both, evaluating audit work, costings and timing in the light of comments from management; evaluating the financial accounting performance of management in the light of comments from the audit firm;

● The NEDs on the committee should have a balance of skills and experience. They should actively promote and encourage the availability of all relevant information to the committee. They should probe sensitively but questioningly;

● Members of an audit committee must recognise (and, incidentally, so too must the remuneration committee) that there is an extra time commitment involved. In times of financial difficulty, or when a major transaction is contemplated, the time involvement can be both heavy and unplanned (in the sense that it will not have been scheduled at the start of the financial year). Even in the 'standard' (no financial difficulty/no major transaction) year, the members of the audit committee should probably expect to meet three or four times a year in addition to their attendances at the normal board meetings. The rate of remuneration for the NEDs on these committees should reflect this commitment and responsibility;

● Audit committees must be firm minded but tactful. Whilst not interfering in the functioning of management, the committee must be prepared to make appropriate enquiries, and challenge the propriety of aspects of financial reports, and the effectiveness of internal control. Tact will be involved in determining how such challenges are communicated to management, discussed and evaluated (in the light of management comments and reactions) and the necessary action taken. The role and effectiveness of the audit committee chairman will be crucial.

In considering the financial reports, the members of the audit committee should have an early involvement in evaluating the completeness of significant financial information prior to its publication. They should also review the annual and interim statements, having particular regard to the continued validity of the going concern basis, the accounting treatment of extraordinary or exceptional items, the impact of change in accounting rules, and any proposed change in the company's accounting principles.

One of the prime tasks of the committee is to review the extent to which non audit services are provided by the audit firm and the nature and quantum of such services.

In due course, the committee should make an assessment and recommend the appointment or reappointment of the auditor. From time to time, it has been suggested that there should (without cause for complaint) be an imposed rotation of audit firm after a specified number of years. This change is suggested so that too cosy a relationship does not develop between the audit firm and the company's financial management. In Spain, there is a compulsory rotation every nine years (see chapter 11).

We are opposed to such a suggestion for the UK because we see benefits in continuity and consistency between audit firm and the company. We do, however, see merit in there being a periodical change of audit partner - and most major firms consider such a change of their own initiative and as a matter of course. If the audit firm does not do so, the audit committee should raise the issue.

If generally adopted, these recommendations should not only emphasise and strengthen the relationship of the board with the auditors, but also enhance the public identification of responsibility between the board and the auditor.

In a substantial number of smaller public companies, and in all but the larger private companies, it may be said that it is not practicable, in terms of the composition of the board, to establish a specific audit committee. Nevertheless, it is important that the board's relationship with the audit firm should benefit from independent contributions and approach from NEDs, and, far from causing the executive directors anxieties as to the creation of a split board, the executive directors should feel comforted that other (non-executive) directors can question, evaluate and review the work of the finance director and his team. No doubt there are some managing directors, sales directors, production directors and so on who would not welcome the finance director questioning, evaluating and reviewing their performance and that of their team.

Fraud

Cadbury repeats that the prime responsibility for the prevention and detection of fraud is that of the board. Such responsibility forms part of the board's delegated management functions and has long been established in law, if not in public perception. A well constructed audit plan should create an environment in which material misstatements are detected and the possibility of fraud reduced. It is virtually impossible to devise a system of general applicability which will detect all frauds, particularly one which involves forgery or collusion by senior management. It is too facile to suggest that detection is enhanced by additional auditing procedures. Statistically this is not proved, and the cost would probably outweigh the ephemeral comfort thought to be provided. Fraud is, in practice, more often discovered, almost by chance, by something 'not quite adding up' during the course of normal routine audit procedures. We support Sir Thomas Bingham's recommendation in his report on BCCI for there to be a statutory duty in the case of the regulated sector (such as banks) for auditors to report fraud to the proper authorities. We do not share Cadbury's reluctance to extend that statutory duty beyond the regulated sector. It will be interesting to see what legislation will be introduced following the Government's acceptance in principle of Sir Thomas' recommendation.

Audit reports

Cadbury makes reference to the proposed changes to audit reports as set out in the consultative paper from the Auditing Practices Board (APB). These proposals, which are part of a wider review of reporting practice, aim to give users of financial statements greater information than normally provided by an audit report. These praiseworthy aims have our full support, and emphasise the need for boards and auditors to address the basic matter of communication. They should avoid misunderstandings and misconceptions and incidentally promote the use of the annual report as a positive means of providing information.

The main changes currently under consideration are the inclusion within the audit report of details as to the respective responsibilities of the directors and of the reporting auditors. An 'expectation gap' has arisen between the legal purpose of the report and users' perception of its meaning and content. We agree with the APB that it is important to dispel any belief that the balance sheet provides a definitive statement of the value of the company's assets and liabilities, or that accounts are or can be stated precisely.

In general, we support the example of an expanded auditors' report set out in the appendix to the new APB Statement of Auditing Standards (SAS600) issued in May 1993:-

Auditors' report to the shareholders of XYZ PLC

We have audited the financial statements on pages .. to .. which have been prepared under the historical cost convention's [as modified by the revaluation of certain fixed assets] and the accounting policies set out on page ..

Respective responsibilities of directors and auditors

As described on page .. the company's directors are responsible for the preparation of financial statements. It is our responsibility to form an independent opinion, based on our audit, on those statements and to report our opinion to you.

Basis of opinion

We conducted our audit in accordance with Auditing Standards issued by the Auditing Practices Board. An audit includes examination, on a test basis, of evidence relevant to the amounts and disclosures in the financial statements, and of whether the accounting policies are appropriate to the company's circumstances, consistently applied and adequately disclosed.

We planned and performed our audit so as to obtain all the information and explanations which we considered necessary in order to provide us with sufficient evidence to give reasonable assurance that the financial statements are free from material misstatement, whether caused by fraud or other irregularity or error. In forming our opinion we also evaluated the overall adequacy of the presentation of information in the financial statements.

Opinion

In our opinion the financial statements give a true and fair view of the state of the company's affairs as at 31 December 19.. and of its profit

[loss] for the year then ended and have been properly prepared in accordance with the Companies Act 1985.

It is, however, important that this allocation of responsibilities does not exaggerate the scope of the audit opinion, which is, of necessity, limited. It has, however, to be recognised that some readers of corporate accounts look first at the audit report (to see if it is in qualified form), then at the name of the audit firm, before looking at the figures.

The role of the auditors is the subject of a recent discussion paper entitled 'The Future Development of Auditing', issued by the APB. This paper has already attracted considerable criticism. However, we believe that all its ideas are worthy of serious consideration. It is too easy to dismiss new ideas as far-fetched or impracticable. But all professions must embrace change and development if they are to continue to provide a valued service.

It is premature to provide any detailed comment on the APB paper. After the ideas have been carefully considered and evaluated, it will remain important to be clear where responsibility for the production of accurate accounts lies (namely with the board). The description of audit responsibilities should not be so enlarged that the simple message to shareholders and other interested parties is blurred or overlooked.

The 'going concern' statement

We agree with the Cadbury recommendation (5.23i) 'that directors should state in their report that the business is a going concern with supporting assumptions or qualifications as necessary', and note the view of Final Cadbury that auditors should report on this statement.

Interestingly, the Working Group (to which we referred earlier in this chapter) seems to have doubts regarding the auditors' reporting for they say in paragraph 7.1:-

> We have recommended that disclosure should be made in the OFR (Operating and Financial Review), since this helps to provide a context for the directors' opinion.
> The OFR is outside the financial statements and therefore there is not a requirement in law for it to be audited. However, the Cadbury Committee recommends that auditors should report on the statement. We recognise that this may cause complications, especially if some of the supporting information is felt to be necessary to an understanding

of the financial statements. Similar problems would arise with disclosure in the directors' report. However, we are confident that a satisfactory solution can be found, which can be put in place once consensus on the appropriate place of disclosure becomes clear.

We share the Working Party's concerns. We believe that directors should be very clear that when accounts are prepared on a going concern basis, that is generally interpreted under present accounting guidelines (SSAP2) as meaning that the company will still be operating for 'the foreseeable future'. This is said to mean six months following the date of the audit report or one year after the date of the balance sheet, whichever is the later. If the auditors are not satisfied on this point, then they should qualify their report accordingly. If the directors cannot be satisfied, they should not attempt to produce accounts that show otherwise. The Working Group goes further than SSAP2 in considering the duration of 'the foreseeable future'. In paragraph 2.14 of their draft guidelines they say:-

> The foreseeable future is at least the period to the next balance sheet date. The foreseeable future should extend beyond the next balance sheet date to the extent that the directors are aware of circumstances which could affect the validity of the going concern basis for the company.

The justification for drawing up accounts on a going concern basis must, in the first place, be a matter for the directors. Over the past few years there have been instances of corporate failure, against a history of an unqualified audit report on accounts drawn up on a going concern basis. We believe that the criteria behind such justification should be subjected to renewed and close scrutiny, and that such criteria should be better defined for the future. A study of the six pages of 'Detailed Procedures' emanating from the Working Group tempts the reader to conclude that so much contemplation (of forecasts and budgets, borrowing requirement, liability management, contingent liabilities, products and markets, financial risk management, other factors and financial adaptability) is called for, that few companies could satisfy **all** the criteria. Few management teams would have time left for positive management of the business. Directors who, cautiously, have doubts about a going concern basis being justifiable (and state so in the accounts) write the company's own death warrant, and, financially, perhaps their own as well.

So we face a dilemma here which could go to the root of corporate existence - that dilemma arguably made more acute if the auditors have to report specifically as to whether or not a 'going concern' is a proper basis of accounting to use. We say 'arguably' because few finance directors, audit committees, and boards will wish to make a decision in any but the most clear cases without involving the auditors in their thought processes.

Auditors must be fully satisfied that the business is a going concern, and will remain liquid for at least 6-12 months after the date the accounts are approved by the board. If the auditors have any hesitation about making this statement, they should, in advance, explain their reasons for qualifying the statement and discuss them with management, the audit committee and then with the whole board.

Auditors' liability

In *Caparo Industries Plc v Dickman & others* (1990) the House of Lords laid down that auditors owed a legal duty of care to the company and to the shareholders collectively, but not to the shareholders as individuals, nor to the third party. *Caparo*, which was a case of immensely complex issues, will undoubtedly have a wide ranging effect. It disposed of the misconception that **anyone** can recover damages against negligent auditors. It also removed the misconception that the audit report is a **guarantee** of the accuracy of the accounts. Nevertheless, the *Caparo* decision does nothing to lessen auditors' duty to use care and skill.

Caparo, and other judgments (e.g., *Morgan Crucible v Hill Samuel Bank and others* (1990)*) run counter to public expectation of auditors having to carry an ever increasing range of responsibilities. Whilst, obviously, it can be argued that the existing matrix of responsibility is too limited, there are substantial problems in extending this matrix without driving every auditing firm out of business.

The 1992 enquiry by Lord Justice Bingham into the supervision of BCCI refers to *Caparo*, and in recommendations 3.40, 3.41 and 3.42 states as follows:-

3.40   Under the law as recently laid down, auditors owe a duty of care to their client company and the whole body of shareholders but not to individual shareholders and not to non shareholding depositors. It has been suggested that auditors should report and owe a duty directly to depositors.

* In this case, the court found there was no duty of care to the hostile bidder in a takeover, although the case was settled before an appeal was heard.

3.41   I take the suggestion to be founded on one or other or both of two propositions. First that auditors would take greater care if such a duty were owed and second that a careless auditor should bear the burden of compensating a depositor who has lost money through his carelessness. The first of these propositions is not self evidently true given the duties an auditor already owes and the discipline to which he is subject. Nor is it established by the facts of the present case since no want of care by any auditor has as yet been shown. The second raises questions of policy (for example the risk of encouraging audit opinions emasculated by qualifications and disclaimers) and practice (for example the cost and availability of insurance).

3.42   This question may well at some point in the future call for consideration in depth. The material submitted to the Inquiry does not lead me now to recommend any change.

This adds additional emphasis to the point we have made above. In the matter of BCCI, the negligence action had been launched by the liquidator against past auditors of the bank for an amount **more than three times the total annual audit fees of the entire United Kingdom accountancy profession.** The figures are illustrative of the enormous potential problem in extending the scope and responsibility for audit work.

7 The company and its financiers

Introduction

The responsibilities of directors towards their various financiers will differ according to the nature of the finance obtained. However, the underlying fundamental for all will be the same, notably choosing the right financier and form of finance for the business proposition, keeping to specified obligations, such as provision of information or agreed financial covenants, and to generally seek to maintain a good relationship as one would for any supplier, customer or employee. Loyalty and trust need to go both ways and directors need to appreciate the environment in which the financier is operating in order to help them build a sound relationship with them.

When a company has a need for additional finance, it will usually turn to its existing bankers and this chapter concentrates on the relationship between the company and its bank financiers. However, it may be that the company had reached the limit of its ability to raise bank finance and therefore needs to look further afield and is worth considering the principal sources of alternative funding.

Equity capital

Equity capital is the main source of finance in the absence of further bank lending. Public companies working with their corporate broker will look to issue new shares to existing shareholders through the Stock Exchange. This process is called a rights issue. Rights issues are regulated by the London International Stock Exchange and the company's advisers will be experienced in managing such issues.

Existing shareholders will be the most obvious and, indeed, the easiest source of finance for unquoted companies. However, existing shareholders may no longer have sufficient funds or appetite for further investment and the company may need to turn to new sources of equity investor.

The Financial Services Act 1986 has brought additional regulations to the process of approaching potential new shareholders. In summary, it is not possible to approach individuals without an investment advertisement which has been approved by a person authorised to conduct investment business. An investment advertisement may also be required by the prospectus requirements of the Companies Act 1985. The importance of appropriate legal advice is obvious.

It is possible to approach a small number of private equity institutions who are more commonly known as venture and development capital houses. Providers of development capital seek to invest in relatively high risk unquoted companies to finance growth. In return they will require a relatively high rate of return for their investment - typically compound return of in excess of 30% per annum. The development capitalist will conduct a thorough review of the business and prospects of the company but will be especially interested in the quality of the management team, the company's track record and the market within which it operates. Dealing with one or two development capital houses can be a much easier process than attempting to raise funds from a wider population although the development capitalists will require a number of legal agreements to protect his investment and will, usually, seek representation on the board of directors.

Mezzanine finance

The risks and rewards of mezzanine finance lie mid-way between bank finance and equity capital. Mezzanine finance will be treated as a loan in the company's financial statements and are often secured by a second charge of the company's assets, subordinated to senior bank finance. The mezzanine financier receives his return in two ways: firstly, through floating rate interest on the loan; and, secondly, through rights to a small percentage of the ordinary shares of the company which are exercisable at some point in the future. These rights are more commonly referred to as an 'equity kicker'. The overall level of return required by a mezzanine financier is likely to be in the region of 25% compound per annum.

Bank lending

As the main financiers to a business, banks cannot be categorized as just another supplier. They have an unique role to play in the life of a business, sitting somewhere between equity investors and trade suppliers. They provide working capital to a business, in the shape of loans, overdrafts and trade finance enabling it to function and to trade.

Their risk profile is also unique. Although their analysis of the risks involved in a business would be similar to that of a potential equity investor, by virtue of holding charges over company assets they become preferred creditors. In exchange for this potential benefit, banks customarily receive smaller margins for their finance than would venture capitalists, mezzanine providers or shareholders.

It is worth examining in some detail, the unique nature of the relationship between companies and their bankers, their responsibilities towards each other and the banking environment in which these relationships will be maintained during the 1990s.

The 1990s banking environment

The banks' conflicting roles

If a company is negotiating a loan with a bank, some understanding of the bank's situation is helpful. Britain's banks are in an unenviable position. As widely held, joint-stock institutions with the same commercial pressures as their customers, they also have a duty to their shareholders to maximise profits and minimise risk.

In addition to this commercial role, they are looked to for succour for the economy through support for business during a downturn. They are expected to play a lead role in economic recovery through maintaining lending to stimulate consumer demand, or lending for reinvestment for economic and export growth. This support must be provided within a framework of prudent and profitable lending.

Banks also have a 'quasi fiduciary' role to play in providing money market mechanisms. In this role, they are subjected to the effects of Government monetary policy in that they must pass on interest rate rises to their customer base, regardless of the customer's ability to pay and regardless of the interest rates prevailing at the time the loan was made. Such increases may, of themselves, trigger a default on a loan which could otherwise have been satisfactorily discharged.

In addition, banks are the subject of regulation in terms of capital adequacy requirements, which in themselves determine the amount of lending the banks can entertain.

The Bank for International Settlements demanded a capital to assets (i.e., loans) ratio of 8% to be in place by the end of 1992. This has exacerbated the worldwide credit crunch already precipitated by Third World debt defaults, UK bad debts, the cost of restructuring of Eastern Europe and the retrenchment of Japanese and US banks caused by their domestic problems.

There are two main consequences of these capital-adequacy requirements:-
- they may restrict the banks' ability to pay the dividends commercially necessary to maintain shareholder support; and
- the banks will seek higher rewards, in the shape of increased margins, for the commitment to borrowers with limited capital resources.

This duality of responsibility does not mean that the banks have an impossible task, nor does it suggest that they are beyond criticism should they fall short of expectations. In the past, they have often deserved the soubriquet of 'fair weather friends', when acting in their own commercial interests during times when counter-cyclical behaviour would be more beneficial to their customers.

The banker as businessman

However, it is worth contemplating the background to a banker's thought processes when viewing his attitude towards his corporate customer. Essentially, when banks weigh up the risks and rewards of each lending decision, there are many factors beyond loyalty to the customer that need to be considered. Due to new capital adequacy requirements and the damage control that is needed on bank balance sheets to remedy imprudent lending, the relationship between corporate customer and banker will have to undergo fundamental changes in the 1990s.

Although bankers are improving their accounting skills, they are not usually trained as accountants and appear to take a somewhat arbitrary view of lending risk. They often fail to get close to their customer, particularly when they are one of syndicate lenders, who rely on guidance and information from a lead bank or a merchant bank as to the creditworthiness of a borrower. Therefore, to a large extent, the banker relies on audited information, which, in the light of recent spectacular business failures, has led directly to the current debate (reviewed in chapter 6) over audit standards and the auditor's duty of care.

Compliance with loan agreements

The calculation of ratios vital to the process of prudent lending, such as liquidity (debtor days, current assets/current liabilities etc) and solvency (leverage, debt gearing, interest gearing etc), all depend on reliable audited or management accounts, both of which depend on effective audits of management and systems on the part of the corporate borrower.

Given the apparent shortcomings in the extent to which a banker can rely on the audit report, the perceived soundness and effectiveness of the management team, and the relationship that can be built with it, have become much more important. If the banker feels that he is dealing with honest and competent management, he will be far more amenable to theoretical shortfalls in arbitrary ratios, and to the occasional receipt of (timely and adequately explained) bad news. He will not appreciate unpleasant surprises springing from inadequate or tardy disclosures.

So companies must be open with the bank, complying to the letter with their obligations contained in the covenants of loan agreements. There is no such thing as a 'technical' breach; all the terms of a loan agreement exist for a good reason. What a corporate customer regards as a 'technical' breach could justifiably be regarded by a bank as a breach of an agreement if the bank is not advised about it. However, the bank if so advised will tend to be more prepared to negotiate favourably with the customer.

Companies will often feel that certain information might potentially be commercially sensitive, or indeed, materially damaging to the customer/banker relationship. This is particularly so when it is a disclosure point that might trigger a breach of covenant, such as a 'material adverse change' in the business which itself is not predefined in loan agreements and can only be based on subjective assessment. Management might be tempted to feel that certain sensitive issues should be concealed from bankers and auditors alike. It is almost always the case that such issues should be raised at an early stage.

Strong corporate governance would send an unmistakable signal to a bank that its inherent concerns over business ethics, checks and balances to the executive function and its standards of disclosure are taken seriously. After all, companies which trade with the help of bank facilities are using bank money to trade, to make profits for their shareholders, and to pay the salaries of employees and directors.

Information and audited accounts

In the main, it is the audited accounts which are used as a primary source to verify compliance with the terms of financing agreements and which enable the completion of a compliance certificate for the banks. They also provide information upon which banks make lending decisions. Banks are therefore becoming increasingly nervous about the extent to which audited accounts can be relied upon for the purposes of compliance, and also the extent to which Caparo and succeeding landmark court judgments have established that auditors do not, as such, owe a duty of care to lenders.

Accordingly, in addition to enhancing their own accounting and investigations capabilities, the banks are seeking through the British Bankers Association (BBA), to obtain guarantees from auditors which go beyond the scope of the traditional audit report, and which establish an actionable duty of care on the part of auditors to the banks.

Discussions between the BBA and the Audit Practices Committee are at an advanced stage and centre on the Caparo ruling that, before a duty of care on the part of the auditor to a third party can exist, any person or persons giving advice or information to a third party must:-

- be aware of the nature of the transaction between the corporate customer and the third party;
- must be aware that the advice or information will be passed to the third party; and
- the third party is likely to rely on that advice or information in making the decision to enter into the said transaction.

Where the assurances required are of a specific nature and concern a specific area (for example, management information systems) or a specific transaction, the bank and auditor can enter into a separate specific agreement. Where it is of a general nature, the existing scope and purpose of an audit and the inherent limitations of the audit report, would be invoked in the refusal of an auditor to issue any kind of undertaking.

The bank as a supplier of finance

The primary responsibilities of banks are in the nature of normal supplier responsibilities - to supply the service being marketed in a cost-effective, timely, efficient and professional manner. They would also be expected to comply strictly with the terms of any loan or other agreement, although these are generally not onerous upon banks. However, due to the unique nature of the relationship between bank and corporate customer, and the vital and often irreplaceable commodity being supplied, the banks have responsibilities beyond those of a normal supplier. Indeed, in the UK many smaller companies look to them as a lender of last resort.

It is the responsibility of all bankers to work alongside and get to know their customers to a far greater degree than would a trade supplier. In order to assess and monitor the degree of exposure he faces, particularly in a downturn, the banker must understand the competitive environment in which his customer operates.

Who is primarily to blame when a business goes under and bankers incur bad debts? Is it the bank for imprudent lending or the borrower for imprudent borrowing? It is a moot point, but what is often at question is the extent to which the banks' lending decision was based on full disclosure of the financial condition (then and prospectively) of the borrower.

Many directors now see banks as protagonists rather than colleagues, an attitude engendered by the competitiveness of the banking market in the 1980s. Companies were then able to shop around for the finest lending margin and banks were prepared to cut their margins in order to win or retain business. Both bankers and companies promoted the concept of transaction-oriented banking at the expense of building up their relationships.

With asset values then increasing faster than the rate at which interest accrued, security or asset-backing for the lending was not regarded as a problem.

However, the onset of recession in 1989 changed all that, with dire consequences for banks and borrowers. Recession revealed the extent to which banking relationships had weakened and the lack of trust which had often developed. Directors either failed to keep their bankers fully informed of the real state of the company's affairs, or indeed may not have been aware how fast asset values were falling. Bankers responded by being unhelpful and resisting customer requests for more facilities or for waivers of covenants. Frequently bankers required their corporate customers to commission, at the customer's expense, a financial review by an independent accountancy firm nominated by the bank. Typically, the nominated firm would have a strong insolvency department, and the same firm would be the obvious choice for the bank to choose as receivers should the customer's refinancing request be turned down. Accounting firms would have found it difficult to resist the temptation to present the financial review on anything but a pessimistic basis leading to the inevitable but lucrative receivership appointment.

It is interesting to note that one of the clearing banks has recently taken the decision in the light of public criticism to appoint receivers who were not involved in the investigating role. Furthermore, such receivers are also required to tender their price in advance.

Entrenched positions developed until neither side trusted the other, leading to the possibility of sudden withdrawal of support by the bank due to lack of trust, or the company lending unexpectedly going bad. Some bankers took the view that the vast majority of business problems were uniquely attributable to bad management and that good, well run businesses did not fail in a recession. Experience has shown that it is recessions which expose badly managed businesses and therefore are the last straws which kill off a business.

A good working bank relationship should be built over the long term, based on the bank trusting the corporate customer and its management and feeling secure with the degree and accuracy of both audited and non-audited information emanating from it. In return, the directors must accept that the bank is entitled to make a reasonable profit from its activities and occasionally, to review its risk profile and exposure to the corporate customer. Such a relationship would allow any problems that might develop to be dealt with on the basis of complete mutual trust.

In order to address recent criticisms of acting arbitrarily towards their customers, some banks are now promoting 'glasnost' in the form of the publication of 'charters' or 'codes of practice'. These are overdue and welcome developments, particularly in the area of interest and commission charges.

The bank - lender, investor, or 'shadow director'?

Fears have been expressed that, should a very close relationship develop between banker and corporate customer, there is a risk that the banker might effectively become a 'shadow director', telling management what it can and cannot do, but without full accountability. Such fears are exacerbated by the formal or informal evolution of a 'lead banker', a situation which is more and more common both through formal syndication of debt or through the 'London Approach'.

However, fears of incurring liabilities through acting as 'shadow directors' have receded since the judgment in the M C Bacon case in 1990 indicated that bankers would need to go far beyond the realms of 'norma' banking activities before being at any significant risk.

It is often asked, particularly in the press, why it is that UK banks are so opposed to providing part of their financing through subscription for equity shares in their customers? Although this does occur in the UK from time to time, it is nowhere near as common as it is in economies generally regarded as being highly successful, such as those of Germany, Japan and the USA.

UK banks, excluding UK merchant banks, are likewise reluctant to seek the appointment of one of their own executives to the board of a customer. This may be out of modesty bred of a realisation that bank officials lack a broad enough business training or professional experience to make them effective NEDs. Remedying this shortcoming might have many incidental benefits for bankers in their own banking work.

Perhaps the banker as director works better abroad. Also, it is common in Europe for senior executives to rotate through the major constituent parts of an economy. Such secondment experience in fields as diverse as manufacturing and service industries, the professions and even the civil service and local authorities must serve to improve communication and understanding. Yet a banker's ability to understand and relate to a customer's problems, and the customer's ability to understand and relate to the banker's problems, must greatly improve the chances of fertile co-operation developing between banker and borrower.

Choosing the right mix of banks

Throughout the 1970s, most companies developed a strong relationship with a major bank, which would have provided all major financing needs. However, as banking became more competitive through global overcapacity in the mid 1980s, and as professional treasurers sought to reduce costs and margins, companies tended to develop multiple lending relationships. Unfortunately, when customers needed to restructure or renegotiate their global facilities, the absence of a natural 'lead' bank made it a difficult process. The so-called 'London Approach' (or 'London Rules') evolved with the encouragement of the Bank of England, as a standard response to a lending or restructuring crisis. A lead bank, if not already in place, or Bank Steering Committee, is put in place and a temporary standstill is negotiated with the company which involves crystallizing the existing bank facilities to the extent that they have been drawn down. Further cash required to keep the company going in the short term is then negotiated with the lead bank or steering committee, even if the amounts were within the existing facility amounts.

For a company to have too many banks must raise concerns about security, gearing, covenants, debt servicing and disclosure. Too few banks would leave companies exposed to the vagaries of their individual lending policies, balance sheet and ancillary service capabilities. A mix of banks is preferred, consisting of:-

- at least one clearing bank to provide:-
    - clearing banking;
    - a contender for lead or merchant bank;
    - some wholesale lending; and
    - ancillary services.

- a small number of wholesale lenders (some UK, some foreign):-
  - as alternative lender to the clearer (particularly for non-sterling borrowings); and
  - to provide competition on ancillary services.

- possibly, an independent merchant bank for specialist advice and for specific projects (e.g., acquisitions and disposals).

A transparent banking and lending structure will help reassure all lenders that the company can be trusted.

Choosing the right mix of debt

UK companies tend to rely more than their overseas competitors on equity investment coming through from highly sophisticated and liquid stock markets. UK companies often fail to structure their debt to match their assets, or working capital cycles or project needs.

Too much short term debt is generally carried by UK companies, arising both from their desire to be flexible and from the relative lack of long term sterling finance available. This market has suffered from the 'crowding out' effect of past heavy issues of Government borrowing, which is obviously less risky for an investor than long term corporate debt.

It is clear from the events of the 1980s that if bankers behave towards customers as fair weather friends only, or if the banks continually receive bad news or unpleasant surprises, good customer/banker relationships cannot be developed. The development of much closer ties, founded in bilateral mutual trust, between companies and their bankers must become the generality rather than the exception.

Banks and companies will need to take a more 'long termist' approach, perhaps through equity holding by banks in order to effect cash conservation by reducing interest payments, mitigating the clamour for dividends from 'short termist' investors and sharing in the long term growth that should follow to the benefit of all.

8 Pension schemes and their governance

Introduction

A comprehensive consideration of good pensions governance is an herculean task. This chapter confines itself to an examination of various aspects of pensions governance following the Cadbury Committee Report and makes various suggestions and recommendations of our own. It highlights some of the areas which are under scrutiny in relation to the Pensions Law Reform Committee under the chairmanship of Professor Roy Goode, and concludes by suggesting issues which we consider companies should address.

Occupational Pension Schemes touch and concern the lives of many people in the UK. It is estimated that 19 million people* in the UK are members or beneficiaries of Occupational Pension Schemes (OPS). The 1970s and 1980s witnessed the growing importance of accrued pension rights as a source of personal wealth. It is reported that if mortgage debts are deducted from the value of personal sector residential dwellings, then the value of accrued Occupational Pension Rights in 1989 was equivalent to about 70% of the wealth reflected by house values.** The 1980s also witnessed the further rise of pension funds as major and influential investors on world stock markets.

Table 1 looks at the overall value of personal sector wealth and shows a breakdown between the aggregated values of owner occupied homes (residential buildings) and accrued occupational pension rights. Table 2 gives the value of pension fund holdings in UK company securities.

* Social Security: The Government's Expenditure Plans 1992-1993 to 1994-1995, CM 1914 1992.
** House of Commons Social Security Committee Second Report: The Operation of Pension Funds.

Table 1

Personal section wealth

£ billion

Year	Residential buildings	Accrued occupational pension assets	Total £ billion
1976	142	50	332
1977	160	65	397
1978	204	90	478
1979	271	120	604
1980	307	150	693
1981	320	180	729
1982	350	215	814
1983	410	255	936
1984	461	295	1,043
1985	527	330	1,167
1986	619	360	1,367
1987	744	401	1,555
1988	1,010	441	1,939
1989	1,097	482	2,187

Source: CSO Baseline, Inland Revenue Statistics Table 114

The figure for the total personal wealth sector and of residential buildings relate to the end of each calendar year whereas the figures for the aggregate value of accrued pension rights is an average value for the year in question. In some years there will be very little difference between the dates of measurements, although in years of high inflation, the figures are not strictly comparable. They are nevertheless a guide to the level, and the changing proportional value, of the main sections of personal wealth.

House of Commons Social Security Committee Second Report: The Operation of Pension Funds.

Table 2

Pension funds: market value of holdings of UK securities

£ billion (cash terms)

31st December	Ordinary Shares	Other	Total
1979	18.0	0.8	18.8
1980	23.8	1.0	24.8
1981	27.6	1.0	28.6
1982	36.0	1.2	37.2
1983	48.4	1.4	49.8
1984	65.4	1.8	67.2
1985	82.3	2.3	84.7
1986	106.1	3.2	109.3
1987	117.5	4.6	122.1
1988	125.8	5.7	131.5
1989	157.8	7.0	164.8

Source: CSO database compiled by the House of Commons Library

It is reported that the market value of shares owned by pension funds rose over eightfold during the last decade and, as the value of pension funds has increased, they have taken a significant share of the ownership of stock market securities. Whereas in 1963, pension funds held 6.4% of the share capital of Stock Exchange listed companies, by 1990 pension funds held almost one third of all quoted shares on the Stock Exchange (31.4%). This made them the most important single group holder of these securities.*

Pension funds or schemes generate considerable interest from all sectors of the economy. Barely a week passes without some scrutiny by the judiciary or by the media of the way in which pension schemes are managed, governed or operated.

* House of Commons Social Security Committee Second Report: The Operation of Pension Funds.

Debates include whether the assets are invested ethically or 'greenly', and, more recently, whether pension scheme assets are sufficiently segregated from the employer's corporate assets to be safe from unscrupulous proprietors of companies, predators or simply from poor managers.

The Cadbury and Goode Committees

Paragraph 4.51 of Draft Cadbury dealt with the issue of pensions governance as follows:-

> 4.51 The security of company pension funds has been highlighted by the Maxwell affair and those responsible for pension fund regulation and legislation are reviewing what action to take to strengthen the security of pension fund assets in the light of the House of Commons Select Committee Report on the matter. It is a complex task of the first importance and one which the appropriate authorities have in hand. The basic corporate governance issue is that the governance of the company's pension fund should be *separate and distinct* from the governance of the company itself. It should be the duty of the boards of companies to ensure that there is that separation and that the assets of pension funds are safeguarded. (our italics)

However, Final Cadbury concluded (in paragraph 4.60) that it would be inappropriate to deal specifically with pension fund governance issues, because such issues fell within the remit of the Goode Committee.

One of the recommendations of the House of Commons Social Security Committee Report on the operation of pension funds had been to call for a review of pensions law to be undertaken.

In July 1992 the Secretary of State for Social Security established the Goode Committee with the following terms of reference:-

> To review the framework of law and regulation within which occupational pension schemes operate, taking into account the rights and interests of scheme members, pensioners and employers; to consider in particular the status and ownership of occupational pension funds and the accountability and roles of trustees to fund managers, auditors and pension scheme advisers; and to make recommendations.

Occupational Pension Schemes

There are two common types of pension scheme: *occupational pension schemes* set up by employers for their employees, to provide income during their retirement (and certain other benefits, e.g., a lump sum on death whilst an employee), and *personal pension schemes* set up by insurance companies to allow employees or the self-employed to fund personal retirement benefits for themselves.

We are concerned here with occupational pension schemes. Personal pension schemes are outside the scope of this book.

OPS may in general be categorized as either 'defined benefit schemes' or 'defined contribution schemes', though there are also hybrid schemes.

A *defined contribution scheme* is a scheme under which the employer and the member pay contributions at a fixed rate. Each member's benefits to be provided at retirement (or death) are determined by the value of the fund created by those contributions, the investment return on those contributions and the annuity rates applicable at the time of his retirement (or death). Such schemes are also known as 'money purchase schemes'.

A *defined benefit scheme* promises the member a defined level of benefit on retirement or death. Most defined benefit schemes are final salary schemes. They usually provide a pension calculated with reference to what the member earned just before he retired, multiplied by the number of years of member's service and multiplied by the particular pension scheme accrual fraction (e.g., one sixtieth).

The member usually contributes a fixed fraction of his annual earnings towards the provision of his benefits. The employer usually undertakes to meet the balance of the cost necessary to ensure that the global benefits promised to all members are provided for.

In the UK, approved pension schemes are usually established under a trust, in order to take full advantage of the tax reliefs available for approved schemes (e.g., the income and capital gains of the scheme are tax-free). The assets in the trust (investments of various kinds plus cash) form the 'separate and distinct' fund out of which the benefits promised are to be met. The adequacy of such a fund to meet such promises is periodically evaluated independently. This evaluation typically takes place every three years, carried out by the actuary to the scheme.

If there is a surplus of funds in the scheme (e.g., because contributions have been excessive and/or the investments have done better than expected), then, subject to Inland Revenue requirements and the provisions of the trust deed and rules, the benefits promised by the scheme may be improved, and/or there may be a return of some past contributions to the employer, and/or the employer may take a so-called 'holiday' from making contributions. Alternatively, there may be a shortage of funds in the scheme, in which event the contributions by the employer may have to be increased.

Crucially, therefore, employees must look to the fund for their promised benefits, not to the employer itself, although employees may have rights under their contract of employment. The Deficiency Regulations (referred to below) also now apply.

It is fundamental that the assets in the fund are kept 'separate and distinct' from those of the employer itself. Those who act as trustees of the pension scheme must do so independently of such employer, notwithstanding the fact that many, if not all, of such trustees may be directors and/or employees of the employer.

It is where these fundamentals are not fully observed that problems arise. This is where the issue of pensions schemes and their governance comes particularly sharply into focus.

Separation of assets

As a consequence of the setting up of pension schemes under a trust, there will (or should) be a complete separation of:-

- the pension scheme assets (investments, accumulated income, contributions from members and from the employer and so on) for which the trustees of the pension scheme are responsible; from
- the assets, income and (importantly) liabilities and obligations of the employer itself.

It is when this vital separation becomes blurred, indistinct, or confused that questions arise - often too late. To understand the implications of this issue it is necessary to examine the dichotomy which exists between 'ownership' and 'control' of the scheme assets.

As we have seen, pension schemes are usually established under irrevocable trust under trust law. Trust law, the concepts of which go back many centuries, has been developed on principles of equity by our courts (there has been relatively little legislative innovation). It was developed primarily to deal with what used to be called 'the landed gentry' and their wish to keep their investments as integrated assets within the family for future generations. Whilst it is this body of law which provides the main legal principles governing pension schemes, questions have been raised (over the last decade particularly) as to whether this particular framework is the most suitable one.

Indeed, this is one of the main issues which is to be considered by the Goode Committee. However, certain aspects of trust law as it affects the governance of pension schemes inevitably arise, and we should deal with them here rather than postpone dealing with them pending the Goode report.

The independent functions of the scheme trustees

Although trustees of pension schemes are the legal owners of the pension fund assets, they hold the assets 'on trust' for the benefit of scheme beneficiaries, and the trustees must administer the scheme in accordance with the terms of the governing trust deed and rules.

Sir Arthur Underhill's classic definition of a trust is worth setting out in this context:-

> A trust is an equitable obligation binding the person (the trustee) to deal with property over which he has control (the trust property) for the benefit of persons (the beneficiaries), of whom he may himself be one and any of whom may enforce the obligation.

The 'trustee' may be a number of individuals, or (and this is particularly prevalent in the case of pension funds) may be a limited liability (trustee) company, formed by the employer for the express purpose of acting as trustee. Typically the trustee company will have small share capital, all of which might (confusingly) be beneficially (but valuelessly) owned by the employer, and there will be a number of directors of the trustee company who (whilst not personally trustees of the scheme - the trustee company is, in law 'the trustee') should be expected to behave to the high standards of ethics, independence and legal propriety and correctness as if they were 'trustees' in their personal capacity. It is where individuals have failed to come up to these high expectations, and have chosen not to adhere rigidly to the principles of separation of assets and functional independence, that problems arise.

Where we refer to 'trustees' in this chapter we are including individuals who are **personally** trustees as well as individuals who are directors of the trustee company.

Duties and powers

A booklet issued in 1992 by the Occupational Pensions Board (OPB) entitled 'Pension Trust Principles' lays down the duties and powers of a pension scheme trustee particularly succinctly. The principal duties are set out as follows:-

- To act in accordance with the trust deed and rules of the scheme and within the framework of the law;
- To act prudently, conscientiously and honestly and with the utmost good faith;
- To act in the best interests of the beneficiaries and strike a fair balance between the interests of different classes of beneficiary;
- To take advice on technical matters and any other matters which the trustees do not understand; and
- To invest the funds.

Although it appears, by operation of trust law, that the required separation between 'control' and 'ownership' has been achieved by the interpositioning of the trustee, this is not the complete picture. It does not take account of one or more of the following matters which may in practice influence the actual situation dramatically:-

Trustees may be employees of the employer

Trustees are often directors or employees of the company which has established the OPS - and there is no legal reason for them not to be trustees, although problems of conflicts of interest can and do arise.

Perhaps an extreme example of this problem is illustrated by an extract from the evidence of Captain Peter Jackson (who was a trustee of the Mirror Group Pension Fund) to the House of Commons Social Security Committee. He described a typical meeting of the trustees of that fund:-

> The style of meetings was that you could be kept waiting around for hours including senior directors and editors of newspapers and suddenly he (the late Mr Robert Maxwell) would whirl in in his shirt sleeves and conduct two hours of business in five or six minutes. You could not raise matters, they were steamrollered through. The helicopter would arrive and out he would go in a puff of smoke and you were left asking what was that... Ultimately if a vote was called Mr Maxwell had the casting vote and he had used it in the past so we tried not to throw things

to the vote but ultimately the power of hire and fire of us was in his hands as it was for all the scheme's advisers.*

The company itself may be the sole trustee or the trustees may be drawn from senior management

Although there are schemes where an employer is also itself the sole trustee of a pension scheme it has established for its employees, this situation is becoming increasingly unusual (it has certainly always been undesirable) and is normally confined to those schemes which comprise insured schemes, individual arrangements or lump sum death benefits only. However, where the employer is the sole trustee a serious conflict of interest may inevitably and predictably arise. There is a similar potential for conflict when directors of the employer are also trustees. Let us illustrate the problems.

A company is managed by its directors, and the directors' specific powers and duties are set out in the company's Articles of Association. Directors have a duty of good faith to the general body of shareholders and must act in the best interests of that general body. Directors also have a duty to consider the interests of the company's employees in general.

However, sometimes the company itself performs the role of trustee or is a corporate director of the trustee company. Then, in addition to the usual trustee duties of honesty and prudence, the trustee directors must act in the best interests of the beneficiaries, acting impartially between all classes of scheme members, including pensioners. The company will, when acting in its trustee capacity, owe a duty solely to them and must act in their best interests **even where this conflicts with the interests of the company itself and its general body of shareholders**. If the company trustee does not act in the best interests of the beneficiaries, it will be in breach of trust. The beneficiaries will then have a right of action to sue the trustee.

Various recent court cases have illustrated just how far the interests of the company and of the beneficiaries may be inconsistent. The problem is obviously exacerbated where the company is a sole trustee. Good governance clearly dictates that the company should not itself be a trustee.

Where the trustees are senior management individuals (which will almost invariably be the case), conflicts of interest and loyalty will still inevitably arise, but such conflicts have to be recognised and managed, perhaps with the help of external professional advisers.

* House of Commons Social Security Committee Second Report: The Operation of Pension Funds

The consultation document issued by the Goode Committee considers the avoidance and management of conflicts of interest. It states that, in relation to almost every pension scheme, there are likely to be some persons with decision making powers who act in more than one capacity. For example, an individual trustee may also be a director of the employer and himself a scheme member. There are also increasing numbers of schemes which have member trustees, and this may cause conflicts too.

Whilst conflicts may be tempered by the presence of other (independent) trustees, it has not been felt to be practicable for there to be a mandatory requirement for there to be independent trustees. This is perhaps because there is not a sufficient number of independent people of the right calibre around to cover all the UK approved pension schemes in existence. There are 167,000 registered OPS in the UK. However, of all OPS members, 90% are encompassed within 10% of the total number of UK schemes. The appointment, as trustees, of **some** of the company's own NEDs should, we suggest, become mandatory for all listed companies.

Powers retained by an employer and their proper exercise

As we have seen, the pension scheme trustees are the legal holders of the pension scheme assets, but they must administer the trust fund in accordance with the provisions of the trust deed and rules of the pension scheme. The trust deed and rules will provide for various powers and discretions to be exercisable by the trustees, or by the employer only, or by the employer and the trustees jointly, in the various circumstances set out in the trust deed and rules.

The usual powers reserved to the employer, by which the employer can retain effective control of the pension scheme, are the power to appoint and remove trustees, to amend the scheme rules; to reduce, suspend or terminate its liability under the scheme, and to include groups of employees from other associated employers.

As the consultation document issued by the Goode Committee also points out, an employer's powers under the trust deed and rules can be very wide and there are few legal limits on the powers the employer may retain under the trust deed. The consultative document recognised that the primary responsibility of an employer is for the financial stability and development of the business on which existing and future employees as well as pensioners depend.

There is no obligation in the UK for an employer to establish a pension scheme at all, or, once established, to continue that scheme indefinitely. A decision to discontinue a pension scheme can have acute industrial relations implications.

Also, as the Goode consultation document points out, the employer has a wide measure of freedom to determine the content of the trust deed and the scheme rules and therefore to dictate the balance of power between the employer and the trustees. However, an employer should exercise the powers it retains under the trust deed and rules reasonably, and not capriciously or for any collateral purpose.

The employer as a beneficiary

It comes as a surprise to many scheme members that the employer can itself also be a beneficiary. The Occupational Pensions Board Guide* describes examples of where the employer could also be regarded as a beneficiary, to whose interests the trustees must also have regard.

In a final salary balance of cost scheme, if the scheme's investments perform well and excess funds emerge, the employer may be entitled under the trust deed and rules to make a temporary suspension of its future contributions or, if permitted, take a payment to the employer from surplus. Therefore, the Guide concludes that the employer may benefit from good investment performance of the fund, and for this reason may be regarded as a beneficiary.

The employer may further be entitled to surplus funds on a winding-up of the scheme.

Ownership of surplus

The consultation document issued by Goode recognised that the scheme surplus problem has been the strongest cause for pension scheme litigation over the last decade. It is this area which most forcefully illustrates the conflicting interests between employers and scheme members, and the pressure placed on trustees to be, and to be seen to be, impartial.

Self-investment

To what extent should pension scheme assets be invested in shares of the employer itself or be utilised for the benefit of that employer (e.g., by purchase and leaseback of the employer's premises)?

It is inevitable that the scheme will be dependent upon the successful performance of the employer for future contributions. Should this dependence be increased by self-investment of past contributions and accumulations?

* Pension Trust Principles, published by the Occupational Pensions Board 1992

The National Association of Pension Funds (NAPF) set up a working party on this issue which reported in 1988. It concluded that '...self-investment is an undesirable practice which creates potential conflict of interests, irresolvable pressures and argument between trustees and company managements'. However, the NAPF finally decided against recommending legislation, but did recommend a code of best practice. The code of practice provided that no new self-investment of any type should be made, except in extreme circumstances. The code also emphasised the necessity for full and meaningful disclosure to members.

Subsequent events, such as the Maxwell case, put enormous pressure on the Government to bring into force the draft regulations it had previously been considering. These were rushed through as the Occupational Pension Scheme (Investment of Scheme's Resources) Regulations 1992. These regulations provide that **not more than 5%** of the current market value of a pension fund's assets may be invested in 'employer related investments'.

'Employer related investments' means shares or other securities issued by the employer, land which is occupied, or used by, or subject to a lease in favour of the employer, property, other than land, which is used for the purposes of any business carried on by the employer, and loans to the employer. The Regulations also provide that, to the extent that any sums due and payable by the employer to the scheme remain unpaid, those sums shall be regarded for the purposes of the Regulations as loans which constitute employer-related investments. There are transitional provisions which allow a scheme to disinvest over a period of two to five years.

Apart from the 5% statutory limitation, trustees are under a general duty to exercise their powers in the best interests of present and future beneficiaries, acting impartially between different classes of beneficiaries. Many major schemes laudably prohibit all forms of self-investment.

In the *Mine Workers' Pension Scheme* case (1984), it was held that where the purpose of the trust is to provide financial benefits for the beneficiaries, the best interests of the beneficiaries are normally their best **financial** interests. Therefore, the power of investment must be exercised so as to yield the best returns for the beneficiaries, judged in relation to the risks of the investment in question and the prospects of the income yield and capital appreciation.

However, in *Evans v London Co-operative* (1976), where the rules of the superannuation scheme conferred upon the trustees express power to lend money to the employer, it had been held that it would be wrong to suppose that the trustees were forbidden to give that employer financial assistance on preferential terms, if the trustees considered that the security of the employment of their members might be imperilled without such assistance being made available.

The central point, then, is whether the investment in the employer is in the interests of the beneficiaries. There may be circumstances where an investment would help to preserve employment. Even if this were the case, the benefit of such a course to all classes of potential beneficiaries, other than current employees, would be less clear.

The consultative document issued by the Goode poses two questions on this issue. Do the present limits on self-investment provide adequate protection for scheme members? Should there be restrictions on investments where any of the trustees, the employer and the scheme advisers have any connection?

Investment management and custodianship

Under the Financial Services Act 1986 (FSA), only authorised persons under that Act may now deal in investments and give investment advice. Section 191 deems pension trustees to be carrying on investment business for these purposes, unless they have delegated the day to day investment decisions to an authorised person. The majority of trustees of self-administered pension schemes are not authorised persons. This precludes them from engaging in day to day investment activities. Therefore, these activities are usually delegated to an investment manager. However, the trustees will retain ultimate responsibility for investment strategy. Investment managers are normally members of IMRO, and are subject to detailed regulation. IMRO's role in the Maxwell affair was much criticised, not least by IMRO itself.

Custodianship is central to the security of pension assets. Unlike the investment management function, custodianship is not a regulated activity. Trustees have a duty of care to beneficiaries to safeguard pension scheme assets. The custodian appointed must be is financially sound, reliable and truly accountable to the trustees.

In the UK, the investment management and custodianship functions may be carried out by the same organisation. This contrasts with the USA, where the practice is prohibited. The anomalies which came to light in relation to the Maxwell pension schemes increased discussions as to whether these two functions should have to be performed by separate organisations. This was one of the areas covered in the consultative document issued by Goode. The NAPF in their response to Goode, dealt with the issue as follows:-

The NAPF believes that the essence of secure custody is the existence of proper systems of control. Provided there are proper controls, there should be no need to separate the custodian from the fund manager. If they are not separate businesses there should, however, be evidence that the two functions are carried out in separate parts of the business. This is essential where there is a link to the employer, for example, in connection with the custody of a bank's or insurance company's own fund.

Information and accountability

Disclosure and accountability are important planks of Cadbury and are also relevant to a discussion on pensions governance. Statutory obligations of disclosure are already placed on scheme trustees. Trustees are required to supply certain information to their members automatically, and to make other information available on request. The responsibility is on trustees and managers of the schemes. The OPB is responsible for administering the legal requirements. The emphasis should surely be on quality and timing of information. The extent to which this is universally achieved in practice is questionable.

The Occupational Pension Schemes (Disclosure of Information) Regulations 1986 impose on all schemes the legal requirement to obtain annually audited accounts and other information which accompanies the accounts. The regulations provide that the trustees must provide a report which generally contains the following items:-

- A trustees' report, which includes certain information as to their appointment and removal and a review by the trustees of the progress of the scheme;
- An investment report containing a review of the investment policies pursued during the year, and a review of the investment performance of the scheme during the year;
- The accounts comprising:-
  - a revenue account showing the income and expenditure during the financial year;
  - a statement of net assets at the end of the financial year at market value;
  - a reconciliation of the revenue accounts and the net assets statement; and
  - a statement as to whether the accounts have been prepared in accordance with Parts 2-4 of the Statement of Recommended Practice 1 (SORP1) issued by the Accounting Standards Committee in May 1986, and if not where there is any material departure;

- A report by the scheme auditor; and
- A copy of the latest actuarial statement.

The regulations apply to each scheme year which commenced on or after 1 November 1986.

Copies of the trustees' report must be made available not more than one year after the end of the scheme year. It must be available on request, free of charge, to members and prospective members, beneficiaries and recognised independent trade unions.

In addition, the trustees are under a statutory responsibility to provide certain prescribed information, for example:-

- documents which constitute the scheme must be open to inspection by members;
- basic information about the benefits, terms and conditions of the scheme accompanied by the name of a contact and address to which enquiries for further information should be sent; and
- information to individuals concerning their own benefits on request, or on the occurrence of certain events or retirements.

The deficiency regulations

Mention must be made of the Deficiency Regulations which became effective from 1 July 1992. Employers became liable to make up deficits in pension funding in certain circumstances.

These regulations apply to all OPS, other than money purchase schemes. If the value of the scheme's liabilities exceed the value of its assets at the time when the employer becomes insolvent, or at the time when the winding up of a scheme commences if earlier, the amount by which the value of the liabilities exceeds the value of the assets is to be treated as an unsecured non-preferential debt due from the employer to the trustees of the scheme.

Good pension scheme governance: an agenda

Some issues (although this is not intended to be an exhaustive list) which companies need to address to achieve good pensions governance include:-

- Is the company the sole trustee of the pension scheme? If so, are there any other suitable persons who could become trustees in its place?
- What training is in place for trustees of the pension scheme? How effective is it? Are the trustees aware of the qualification certificate for trustees operated by the Pensions Management Institute?

- Is there in place a mechanism by which any conflicts of interest arising in relation to the pension scheme can be effectively managed? Has the company identified those areas which are susceptible to conflicts, and decided what action to take to reconcile or at least deal with the various interests? Do the trustees and the company know who has control of the various powers and discretions under the trust deed and rules?
- Do the members of the pension scheme have adequate knowledge of their pension benefits? Is communication effective? Has quantity been confused for quality?
- Is there any self-investment above 5%? If so, what action will be taken to reduce this investment? Even if all self-investment is within the 5% limit, is it in the best financial interests of the members?
- Are there agreements in place which deal with the investment management and with the custodianship of pension scheme assets? Do these give sufficient protection? What enquiries have been made as to the suitability of the investment managers and the custodians to perform their respective tasks? Should these two functions should be performed by separate organisations?

We recommend that the above matters should be addressed by companies (and, where relevant, also by trustees) in relation to their pension schemes to improve the vitally important pensions aspects of corporate governance.

9 Corporate governance and the environment

Background

In recent years, there has been growing public and media attention focused on the environment. Issues such as damage to the ozone layer, the greenhouse effect, carbon taxes, air pollution, the 'sick building' syndrome, waste reduction and management, and contamination of soil and water resources are of great concern to all citizens. Increasingly they are subjects of which headlines are made. Recent surveys undertaken by the European Community, and by both member and non-member states, confirm that the condition of the environment is one of the public's paramount concerns. This is in part manifested in greater international consensus. The pursuit of economic growth must be tempered, and the goal of sustainable development must be substituted for maximization of growth regardless of potential damage to the environment. Worldwide recession may have caused a backlash against the 'green movement', but the trend towards more stringent environmental regulation remains and strengthens. Environmental concerns can no longer be consigned to the category of 'interesting but inessential'.

This change in outlook has been marked by an increasing volume of international agreements and, particularly, of European Community legislation. The general environmental policy of the EEC is set out in Article 130r of the 1957 Treaty of Rome, as amended (for the UK) by the 1987 Single European Act. Paragraph 2 of that Article states:-

> Action by the Community relating to the environment shall be based on the principles that preventive action should be taken, that environmental damage should as a priority be rectified at source, and that the polluter should pay. Environmental protection requirements shall be a component of the Community's other policies.

Under the Maastricht Treaty, environmental concerns will receive more explicit consideration.

The environmental provisions of the EC Treaty are given substance through Directives and Regulations. Among the most significant of recent developments is the long awaited Green Paper on Remedying Environmental Damage, which was published on 14 May 1993.

The Green Paper, though intended to encourage debate, shows a marked preference for a system combining strict liability for certain high risk activities with joint compensation funds, to ensure that there are no 'voids' in the system. Other regulating initiatives relating to air and water quality are also being actively pursued.

The EC Council has established the eco-label awards scheme, and approved voluntary eco-management and audit. These schemes are intended to take advantage of consumer preferences for green products. They allow companies whose products or policies meet certain criteria to be advertised using 'eco' logos, proclaiming the environmental friendliness of those products and their packaging.

In the UK, the publication in September 1990 of the Government White Paper entitled 'This Common Inheritance' and the passing of the Environmental Protection Act 1990 (EPA) and the Water Resources Act 1991 confirm that environmental matters are now firmly on the corporate agenda.

Historically, UK environmental law has focused primarily on protection of human health. Those areas of product liability and workers' health and safety are addressed fairly well by existing legislation. Of particular interest are the 1992 Control of Substances Hazardous to Health (COSHH) Regulations, part of a series of health and safety measures designed to focus greater attention on products and substances which are considered hazardous and in consequence potentially injurious to the worker. Failure to abide by these regulations can have severe consequences for corporate bodies as well as for their directors personally and individually.

Health and safety at work

The Health and Safety at Work Act 1974 ('the 1974 Act'), as updated by the COSHH Regulations, imposes a comprehensive statutory duty on employers to provide for the health, safety and welfare at work of all employees. This requirement is in addition to the common law duty of care for the provision of a safe system of work.

As from 1 January 1993, employers are required to appoint competent safety personnel in order to secure compliance with their existing statutory and common law duties, as well as relevant codes of practice, health and safety regulations, maintenance procedures and applicable British Standards. Risk management generally has become a key corporate priority, involving increasingly heavy responsibility for health and safety of employees.

In formulating corporate risk management policies, it is the duty of employers to take all reasonable steps to comply with official health and safety publications and codes of practice, as well as with legislation. Employers must provide plant and work systems (including arrangements for the safe use, handling, storage and transport of articles and substances), information, training and supervision necessary to ensure 'health and safety', maintenance of a safe place of work and a working environment free of health risks. Employers must regularly review safety policy. In particular, they are now required to make a formal assessment of risks so as to identify the protective measures necessary, and to provide employees (including temporary workers) with health monitoring against occupational hazards. There are stringent requirements under the 1992 Management of Health and Safety at Work Regulations concerning the information to be provided to employees. The 1974 Act specifically provides for the offence of corporate manslaughter (with the possibility of charges being brought against directors and officers personally) - a feature which is also to be found in the EPA. The Employers' Liability (Defective Equipment) Act 1989 and the Employers' Liability (Compulsory Insurance) Act 1969 complete the framework (so far) of employee health and safety legislation - a regime which needs to be considered alongside the emerging body of environmental law in the context of corporate governance.

Developments in UK environmental law

The EPA will greatly expand the scope of the waste licensing system that has existed for nearly two decades. Additionally, a duty of care has been imposed on handlers of waste which has begun the process of raising waste management standards. The need for greater recycling and reuse of waste has been accepted by the Government. Active measures are being taken to achieve these goals, together with that of waste reduction.

Air quality issues are also receiving greater attention. The Clean Air Acts of 1956 and 1968 and 1993 have effectively eliminated the deadly city smogs of the early 1950s. The EPA has additionally established an extensive system of permits for air emissions.

Britain and the European Community have also accepted that the production and use of chemicals that deplete the earth's ozone layer must be phased out. They have committed themselves to a fairly aggressive schedule. The Government is also moving forward with legislation to improve ground level air quality.

European standards for vehicle emissions will help to reduce tailpipe emissions of certain chemicals, and emissions from certain types of other (e.g., stationary) sources. The proposed use of tax incentives to encourage reductions of carbon dioxide emissions should have the effect of reducing emissions of other pollutants into the air.

Changes in the regulation of the aquatic environment are also being made. European Community standards intended to ensure improvements in the quality of bathing waters and waters supporting certain aquatic life have now been implemented, and measures designed to reduce the discharge of urban waste water to the environment are progressing. Efforts to improve the quality of drinking water are also continuing. Stringent water quality standards have been imposed and very large spending programmes to ensure that those standards can be met are presently under way throughout the country.

On the land use front, there is pressure to conserve the countryside, with the support of planning legislation. Schemes, such as City Challenge, have sought to promote urban regeneration. Matters have been complicated by the debate over the requirement for registers of contaminative uses to be compiled by local authorities under the EPA. Recognizing the blighting effect that such listings would almost certainly have, the Government has now reconsidered its proposals for the register.

Planning processes now increasingly incorporate environmental concerns. Since the late 1980s, environmental impact statements have been required in connection with the approval of certain types of development projects. The purpose of the statements is to quantify adverse environmental impacts of a project and to identify measures to mitigate those impacts. Where impacts are deemed to be too great, planning applications can be refused.

Many of these same issues are also of significant concern to the construction industry. The Government has identified the greenhouse effect as the greatest single problem facing the global atmosphere, and has committed itself to reduce the production of greenhouse gases as part of an international effort to address this issue. The need for heating and air conditioning generates a significant quantity of 'greenhouse' gases and consumes large quantities of chlorofluorocarbons (CFCs). Thus, the reduction in generation of those gases and the phasing-out of CFCs will cause wide ranging changes particularly in the building industry.

Energy efficiency has been on the agenda since the oil shortages of the early 1970s, and building regulations have adopted insulation values since the mid 1980s. Commercial pressures for increased efficiency are likely to increase if the proposed carbon tax is adopted.

It is clear that environmental concerns are here to stay and that environmental regulation is likely to grow both in scope and complexity. Similarly, the penalties for non-compliance with environmental laws are becoming more and more stringent.

This in itself underlines the need for directors to stay abreast of changes in this volatile area of the law. In addition, the effect of environmental legislation on trade and competition has to be considered. The use of 'environmental' regulations which have the incidental effect of imposing non-tariff barriers to trade has been the subject of hot debate within both the European Community and GATT. The potential implications of environmental legislation in these areas needs to be carefully considered by directors when making strategic decisions, or when considering how to react to proposed legislation.

The US leads, the UK follows

In the US, there has been a marked trend in recent years towards holding corporate officials personally responsible for violations of environmental laws. This trend is evident in the case of both civil and criminal actions, but is most prominent in the area of criminal prosecution of corporate officers for the wrongdoings of their companies, even where the officers had no actual knowledge of the wrongdoing.

The increased emphasis on personal liability is the result of a number of factors. First and foremost, is the belief of enforcement agencies that the spectre of personal liability, and imprisonment in particular, motivates corporate officials to ensure environmental compliance to a greater extent than does the threat of fines being imposed upon the company. Shifting the risk of non-compliance to the individual decision-maker adds a dramatic further dimension to the cost/ benefit analysis on which corporate decisions are typically made. While the benefits of non-compliance may outweigh the costs when viewed from the corporate perspective, they are unlikely to do so from the perspective of the individual decision-maker, who may be faced with huge personal fines or imprisonment.

A philosophical understanding of corporate versus personal decision-making responsibility would be of little avail to enforcement agencies without the imposition of personal liability. The nature of many environmental penalty provisions and the broad reach of those provisions does so. Many environmental laws, for example the US Comprehensive Environmental Response Compensation and Liability Act, impose strict liability for certain offences. In those cases, the enforcement agency may not need to prove either knowledge or negligence on the part of the corporate official in order to obtain a conviction or impose a penalty. As a consequence, imposing personal liability is greatly simplified.

The scope of environmental penalty provisions under US laws tends to be broad. In certain cases, the laws specifically state that the 'responsible corporate official' may be held liable. In others, liability can be imposed on 'any person' who violates some aspect of the law. Enforcement agencies have argued that these provisions should be interpreted broadly enough to include corporate officials with responsibility for environmental matters and the courts have, in many cases, agreed.

As a result of the increased emphasis on personal liability, corporate officials have begun to focus on environmental compliance, and have developed methods to minimize the risk of non-compliance. Enforcement agencies have been able to influence corporate behaviour. They have sought to do this through the publication of enforcement guidelines. Although intended as guides to prosecutors in the exercise of their discretion, guidelines, such as those issued in 1991 by the Department of Justice in Washington, outline factors that should be considered in deciding whether to prosecute a particular case at all and, if so, whether to proceed with a criminal prosecution or a civil action. High among the list of mitigating factors is the implementation of a corporate compliance plan incorporating certain specific elements. Well advised corporate officials are reviewing these guidelines with a view to their companies taking steps to ensure that the mitigating factors described are incorporated into corporate policy.

Corporate governance

We now turn to the impact of environmental legislation on corporate governance.

The framework in which corporate entities now operate is far more formally regulated than in the past. Those companies which transgress the strict provisions of the legislation now leave themselves open to prosecution and the payment of substantial fines for non-compliance. Coupled with the increasing regulatory framework is the requirement that companies should be held responsible for their own polluting actions - the oft quoted 'Polluter Pays' principle. This stricter regime is also reflected in the move away from fault based offences to strict liability offences. Thus, to achieve a successful prosecution, the regulatory authorities no longer need to establish any intent, deliberate or otherwise, on the part of the offending party.

Legislation such as the EPA is structured so that a director or other officer of the company to whom responsibility for the company's environmental compliance has been delegated may be made personally liable for any environmental offences committed by the company. This statutory imposition of liability - also reflected in the Water Resources Act 1991 and the 1974 Act - reflects an increasing trend on the part of the regulators to bring to account those directors or officers who are responsible for the company's environmental compliance and who, to date, have sought to hide behind the corporate veil.

A successful prosecution of a company for an environmental offence will still have an overall impact at board level. Whilst fines in the Magistrates Court may currently not exceed £20,000, there is no maximum limit on the fines which may be imposed on a company in the Crown Court. The amount of any fine, and the attitudes of the court in which the prosecution is brought, will clearly be influenced by the severity of the offence and the former compliance record of the defendant company. Notwithstanding the overall financial standing of a company, it is likely that the board will be further called to account by its shareholders for its action or inaction, and in particular to explain if and why insufficient management controls existed to prevent the company from incurring such a liability.

Whilst a fine may cause short term funding problems for the company, it is the medium to long term effect on sales arising from consumer hostility which are harder to quantify and to counter. The strength of consumer power is well illustrated by the immediate effect on the sales of Exxon's products after the adverse consumer reaction to the Exxon Valdez disaster.

Although the financial risks to the body corporate will help to ensure that directors consider carefully matters of environmental compliance, it is the risk of incurring personal liability and the possibility of imprisonment which will increasingly deter the indifferent director who fails to ensure implementation of appropriate environmental management controls. Under the terms of the EPA, a director may become personally liable in one of two ways. He may incur specific statutory liability for the offences committed by the company, and further a director may be held to be primarily liable for an environmental offence.

Section 157 of the EPA expressly extends any liability of a company for a breach of the provisions of the Act to any 'director, manager, secretary or other similar officer of the body corporate or a person who was purporting to act in such capacity' who consented to or connived to breach the Act or whose neglect allowed an offence to take place.

There is nothing particularly novel about this particular type of offence which has been in existence in a similar form in s37 of the 1974 Act and s87 of the Control of Pollution Act 1974. The difference now is that the regulatory authorities are increasingly inclined to make use of this provision, particularly in the sphere of environment protection. This was evidenced by the six months' prison sentence imposed on a director of a waste disposal company in October 1992 for failing to dispose of special waste in accordance with the requirements of the Control of Pollution Act 1974. The relevant regulatory authority is entitled to pursue those directors or senior managers of the company in circumstances where there have been flagrant breaches of the law or where the severity of the offence committed by the company demands action against a specific director.

Case law in respect of such statutory provisions has established that a director consents to the commission of an offence by the company when he is well aware of what is going on and agrees to it. In the case of connivance, a director will be personally liable if he has knowledge of the course of conduct likely to lead to the offence but, whilst not actively encouraging it, does nothing to prevent the offence from occurring.

Neglect, on the other hand, implies a failure to discharge a duty that the director knows or ought to know he is obliged to perform. In establishing neglect, and in particular a breach of the duties of an individual director, the courts will consider the nature of the company's business and the distribution of its work between members of the board. Clearly, those directors who have direct responsibility for ensuring the company's environmental compliance are those most at risk. Likewise, managers of individual sites or managing directors of subsidiary companies may well find that they, too, are fixed with the necessary responsibility.

The extent to which a 'manager' may be personally liable for breaches of statutory duty was recently considered in the case of *R v Boal* (1992). There a prosecution was brought under the provisions of s23 of the Fire Safety Precautions Act 1971 against an assistant manager of a well known book store. Although on the facts of that particular case, the court decided that the assistant manager in question did not have sufficient control over operations to hold him liable, the dicta of the court indicate that managers may well be liable under other circumstances. Because s23 is analogous to certain sections of the EPA, the Boal decision will help determine the scope of managers' liability under that Act.

Under s157 of the EPA, a regulatory authority may take direct action against an errant director without first commencing proceedings against the company, although in these circumstances in order to gain a conviction against a director, the elements of consent, connivance or neglect will need to be established.

Liability, under s157 may also be incurred 'as a director, manager, secretary or other similar officer of the body corporate'. Moreover, under s158, where an offence committed by one person is due to the act or omission of another person, that other person may be convicted of an offence regardless of whether proceedings are taken against the first person. Shadow directors (possibly being such 'other person') must also give careful attention to environmental matters or risk personal liability. Those directors who have been convicted under s157 or s158 may also be disqualified from being a director under the Disqualification Act.

Many of the provisions of the environmental legislation have been expressed so that they provide that 'any person' who commits a specified act shall be guilty of an offence. Whilst such a provision is principally aimed at corporate entities, it is nevertheless possible for a director or manager of a company who performs the prohibited act to be guilty of an offence. For example, under s85 of the Water Resources Act 1991, a person may be guilty of an offence 'if he causes or knowingly permits any poisonous, noxious or polluting matter or any solid waste matter to enter any controlled waters'.

The verb 'causes' does not presuppose any intent or negligence on the part of the director, but it does, however, require some positive participation on his part, or sheer knowing neglect. Where the defendant director's role is entirely passive, as may be the case where board members collectively decide not to prevent the commission of an offence, then the director may not have 'caused' an offence. He may, however, still be liable for 'knowingly permitting' the commission of the offence. In broadest terms, a person 'knowingly permits' the commission of an offence when he expressly or impliedly authorizes the acts or omission causing the offence. In this context, the term 'knowingly' has been construed as referring to knowledge of the release of poisonous, noxious or polluting matter into controlled waters, and not to knowledge that such a release was contrary to the terms of the relevant discharge consent required under the terms of the Act.

Additionally, many environmental statutes provide that where a corporation is managed by its shareholders, those shareholders shall be liable for acts and defaults in connection with their management of the corporation to the same extent as directors would be liable. The apparent purpose of this provision is to impose on parent companies criminal liability for the acts of a subsidiary where the parent has connived in, or consented to, the offence. Thus, parent companies which seek to shelter their environmental problems in a subsidiary company may not be able to hide behind the corporate veil.

A director may also be liable if he aids, abets, counsels or procures the commission of any indictable offence (i.e., an offence which is triable in the Crown Court), whether the same be an offence at common law or by virtue of any statutory provision. In such a case, the director concerned will only be vulnerable if he had knowledge of the essential matters which constitute the offence.

A director could also be liable for conspiracy if he were a party to a decision made by two or more parties to perpetrate an unlawful act. Various commentaries suggest that the law of conspiracy is unlikely to be used except in very serious cases where the company's directors have agreed quite deliberately to flaunt environmental controls (e.g., in order to save expenditure).

Where an injunction has been granted against a company in the civil courts as a result of a breach of environmental laws, or an undertaking has been given to the court on the company's behalf, the company will be guilty of contempt if it knowingly fails to abide by the injunction or the undertaking. A director of a company who is aware of the terms of the injunction or undertaking is under a duty to ensure that it is obeyed. If he wilfully fails to discharge that duty or ignores it, then he may be punished for contempt. This happened in December 1992 when a director was convicted of contempt and imprisoned for three months for breach of a court order concerning the illegal deposit of waste contrary to the provisions of s3 of the Control of Pollution Act 1974.

Environmental issues and accounts

Directors have an obligation to ensure that the value of the company's assets is not overstated in its accounts. Where actual or potential environmental liabilities are known about, whether affecting real estate, physical assets or intangibles, the assets must be valued and written-down accordingly and/or a provision reflected in the accounts. Major uncertainties may arise because environmental valuation techniques are still evolving. The accounting profession still has to tackle this specific issue substantially.

The board has a responsibility to ensure that the directors' report and accounts present a 'true and fair view' as at the accounting date. If they have reason to believe that any part of the company's assets could be adversely and materially affected by actual or potential liabilities for environmental matters, they will need to ensure that this is reflected either by a downwards revaluation of the asset or assets in question, by making provisions, by a suitable note to the accounts, or by a combination thereof.

It is arguable that the board should periodically commission an environmental audit of the company's facilities for this purpose - and not only from the point of view of considering 'going concern' criteria. Essentially, environmental liabilities are no different from any other liabilities - they may be actual or contingent and can only be evaluated on the basis of proper professional advice.

Interestingly, the draft guidance for directors of listed companies produced by the Going Concern Working Group (to which we referred in chapter 6) included within the criteria to be considered whether the company has a current or potential liability for environmental 'clean up' costs.

We have said above that it is 'arguable' that the board should commission environmental audits. Inevitably, such an audit might produce information about problems of which neither the board nor the environmental authorities were aware. Bearing in mind what we have said about strict (no blame) liability, the availability of injunctions, and the liability of directors, we have no doubt that few boards should or would wish to live in continued ignorance. Neither have we any doubt that any new candidate for a seat on the board should, prudently, satisfy himself as to the company's environmental record and cleanliness (see our pre-appointment checklist for directors in appendix D).

Whilst there is no duty to inform the environmental authorities as to the outcome of an audit commissioned by the board, their awareness of what it might have said may be prompted by remedial work being done or by what is said in or revealed by the accounts. This is a risk - albeit a mitigating one, provided something is done. No board of directors should fail to take appropriate steps to remedy such problems as emerge from an environmental audit, for then actual knowledge followed by inaction clearly leaves them (and the company) in a yet more vulnerable position than had the directors remained in collective and corporate ignorance.

Other than finding out about environmental problems and taking due steps to remedy them, what else can directors do to cushion their vulnerability? Although there is, in general, a growing market for directors' and officers' (D&O) insurance, it is impossible for reasons of public policy for cover to be provided for criminal fines (as opposed to the costs of defending criminal prosecutions).

Also, it will be found that the typical D&O policy excludes liability on the part of the insurer in respect of 'any claim which arises out of seepage, pollution or contamination of any kind'. Insurance policies generally exclude the consequences of claims arising out of or connected with injury, sickness, disease on death, or environmental matters generally.

Neither can insurance be bought to compensate for a jail sentence or for the consequential loss of earnings - whilst 'inside' or in the future thereafter.

Pointers for the future

The environment, including issues of health and safety, will increasingly feature as an important element in good corporate governance. There will be increased pressure on companies to institute environmental audit/management systems. This pressure will be driven by a combination of political and market forces (from both consumers and the financial sector which is trying to reduce its potential liability). There will be an inexorable move towards strict liability, and few hiding places for directors, officers and other employees seeking to avoid personal responsibility for breaches of environmental law. If remedial action is needed, it must be taken sooner and not later. The costs and liabilities should rightly fall on the company, rather than the directors personally. But directors should not rest in ignorant idleness hoping that problems will never emerge or, if they do, will simply go away.

They won't.

10 The role of communications in corporate governance

The positive and important role of communications in corporate governance is admirably summarised in paragraph 3.2 of the Final Report from the Cadbury Committee:-

> An open approach to the disclosure of information contributes to the efficient working of the market economy, prompts boards to take effective action and allows shareholders and others to scrutinise companies more thoroughly.

Given the fundamental precept of this book, namely that the board runs a company on behalf of the shareholders (its owners), what communication functions should board members expect to fulfil? In the context of improved corporate governance, are the current levels of communication too limited? How can these levels be redressed within the limits of confidentiality, the fear of creating false markets, the legal requirements on what constitutes insider knowledge, and the perceived restraints on directors' freedom of speech?

In today's climate, an open approach to communications is seen as a good thing, in the same way that adopting conservation policies, espousing customer and staff care, and going for quality assurance standards, are all seen as positive attributes. Cadbury states that the principles on which their Code of Best Practice are based are '...openness, integrity and accountability'.

Most large corporations are already aware of the need for an overall communications policy, which supports a planned corporate image, supported by a consistent approach to advertising, PR, media relations, marketing, community and staff relations. Together these build a corporate identity which influences both the impression formed of a company by its various audiences and the action it takes as a result. The board has a vital role to play in the whole communications policy and process. The board will develop its own communications needs and audiences. It should provide a critical link between the internal activities of the company and its external audiences, including its own shareholders, both in a proactive and reactive role. The ideal corporate communications plan should therefore make the board the pivotal part of the whole.

Communication links

The board should communicate in several directions, internally and externally.

Board member to board member

Board meetings, however well documented in advance, will rarely provide sufficient communication between directors. Regular briefings or bulletins based on relevant extracts from press coverage, in-house communications and printouts from management information systems should regularly be distributed. Advance notes on issues to be raised and progress reports on board decisions taken should also be issued.

Regular communication helps build confidence between board members and line management.

It also helps to create an united, coordinated and centralised response to media enquiries. The chairman has a key role to play in acting as the company's spokesman, and other directors should not generally usurp this role.

Board to management: management to board

It is especially difficult in large companies for board members to keep abreast of day-to-day management issues. Building a system of regular informal briefings and 'early warning' methods within the confines of commercial prudence should be part of the communications planning process. Ways which have been found to be useful in maintaining contact with management include:-

● greater attention to **accountability** for management communications, including the cultural and political background and an awareness of realistic and accepted expectations;

● assigning responsibilities and duties as appropriate, and ensuring that those responsibilities are understood, accepted and adhered to;

● more selective and disciplined presentation and use of management information systems by the board, and a tighter briefing to the board from those who are responsible for management information systems. Clarity should take priority over quantity;

● ensuring attention is paid to the **upward** flow of communication within the organisation. A 'cascade' always works more naturally **down** a company and much less effectively upwards. Consequently, the upward flow requires much greater, and more consistent, management attention and encouragement;

- electronic media (such as video conferencing) for communication with outlying areas of the organisation, particularly abroad. Such communication should follow the circulation in advance of supporting papers which should enable wide ranging though disciplined discussions and explanations to take place.

Board to shareholders

Every director is under an obligation to ensure:-
- that information which might reasonably be expected materially to affect market activity in, or the price of, the company's shares is released immediately to the Company Announcements Office of the London Stock Exchange;
- that information reaches all shareholders and the market simultaneously;
- the avoidance of a false market in the company's shares.

This crucial level of communication will depend for its success upon the format and style of the annual report and accounts and the arrangements for the annual general meeting. Every other level of communication will precondition the extent and timing of the information to be provided to shareholders.

The annual report should be as comprehensive and open as possible. It provides a valuable opportunity to explain to shareholders and the public what the company is trying to achieve, what it has achieved, and how top management functions are delegated. The workings of the board and its committees should be explained, with details of membership, and each individual board member's background. Some companies, such as Guinness plc in its 1993 report and accounts, anticipate this suggestion admirably.

Certain statements, some of which are requirements under the Companies Act, should be considered carefully, and should clearly indicate company policy on the various issues involved. Statements about community relations, employee involvement and environmental issues are all welcome, but should be substantiated: fine intentions never saved a rain forest or helped to motivate employees. Shareholders are consumers in their own right, and are (rightly) increasingly jaded about vacuous and cynically motivated claims to occupy whichever moral high ground happens to be most fashionable at the time the annual report is produced. Annual reports and accounts should be attractive to the reader. The inclusion of relevant photographs adds interest, and helps shareholders to understand the company's activities better.

Board to public/press

There is an overwhelming temptation for companies to adopt a passive, defensive stance in relation to the press, responding only under pressure and volunteering nothing. But the press can, and should, be used in a positive way. It is surely better for companies to publicise promptly (when appropriate so to do) their own authoritative message than for there to be partly informed, sometimes rumour-driven, speculation by the press which might demand correction, denial or confirmation by the company concerned, which will always look defensive and reluctant. If press comment is wrong or unjustified, as opposed to merely ventilating market rumours, the company may feel obliged to respond to ensure a false market in its shares is not created. Listed companies have obligations under the Yellow Book to publicise important information at an early stage.

There is always a host of excuses for companies not to communicate, some of which may be valid: 'We have had a bad quarter, but orders in hand for the next quarter are so good it would be misleading to talk about the immediate past quarter'; 'Well, we are in talks, but we do not wish to prejudice their success by a premature announcement'; or simply 'We do not yet want to say anything, because anything we say now might be misleading'.

These reasons will not, however, prevent the media from saying something. The press will come up with its own views if newsworthy, right or wrong.

Companies must make sure the media has the correct information from which to form those views, and take steps to influence them fairly but positively. There is seldom press smoke without there being a flame of underlying fact somewhere. Corporate reaction, of some sort, is often therefore called for. 'We never comment on press speculation' and/or 'When we are ready to make a statement, we will do so' are the 'boiler-plate' responses, but how much better it is, where possible, to take the initiative and to communicate the right story.

Board to key groups

All communications will also, however, whether the board specifically intends it or not, have an impact on suppliers, customers, consumer lobbies, buyers and local communities. The range of such communication is vast. It includes:-

- corporate advertising (and sometimes product advertising as well);
- other marketing activity;
- customer services standards;

- supplier relationships (and the extent to which a genuine two-way relationship is established);
- product packaging.

In all of these, a consistent image should be portrayed, and a consistent story told. Nothing undermines the credibility of the board in the minds of its public more than to see contradictory messages coming out of the same organisation.

The board also has a communications role to play in its interface with industry and professional bodies, local and national government, statutory authorities, and potential recruits, existing staff and workforce, and political and ethical lobbies.

Types of communication

The media

There are two main ways in which media communications play a vital role in a company's fortunes. They both demonstrate why media relations should be considered an essential part of the structure and development of corporate governance.

Any company is both a conductor and reflector of media communications. As a conductor, putting out its own messages to the City, to shareholders, customers and the public at large, the company has the opportunity to initiate the news accurately and positively to create and improve its markets and its competitive position. It can influence everything from its net worth to its recruitment attraction in the annual 'milk round', and its corporate successes and image generally.

As a reflector, it will mirror media attention. If it does this in the right way it will enhance its efforts as a conductor. If it simply rejects media attention as an unwanted intrusion or sends back hostile or inaccurate responses, much of the quality of the news it seeks to promulgate will be undermined.

Even a hostile press can be a catalyst for change. It can exert pressure on corporate bodies, forcing them to take the right action to improve. If companies can usefully learn from media communication (which is often in itself a reflection of public attitudes) then much can be achieved.

As a conductor, the importance of communications in creating markets is critical and calls for a co-ordinated and consistent plan, to be echoed throughout the following media channels:-

- advertising;

- public relations, including all external corporate publications such as annual reports, corporate brochures, press releases and public statements;
- internal employee communications, including the company newsletter and information to pension fund members;
- recruitment communications;
- particulars of products and services offered.

In the reflective role, spontaneous press comment can - and often does - excite corporate and indeed also shareholder reaction. Press comment often serves a valuable and incidental benefit in providing the script for shareholders' questions at the AGM.

There is a pleasing symmetry to these conductor and reflective roles, and one which is not coincidental. They throw light on areas that some would rather keep unseen, and force change and greater openness. They can provide the most visible manifestation of how seriously corporate governance is being taken by the organisation concerned.

As a catalyst for change, media pressure has amply demonstrated how the whole communications process can work in improving standards of corporate governance. Each time the press comes close to revealing the truth, as they see it, they risk an injunction being obtained prohibiting further revelations. This is an example of the difficulties the press sometimes face in revealing information in the public interest. The hue and cry raised by the press can be instrumental in increasing concern in the minds of all.

The media can fulfil a useful function in providing objective reporting and well informed commentary on corporate affairs. This role is one which needs to be supported and encouraged as part of the vigilance we should continually maintain - particularly when our Stock Exchange lacks the manning, resources and bloodhounds found in the SEC in America.

Companies can, however, attempt, with varying degrees of success, to use public relations machinations to influence the way in which the press report their situations. While reputable public relations activity can be actively helpful in the way it facilitates communication between companies and the press, attempts to curb or twist media coverage are to be deplored. The media can be one of the strongest safeguards and promoters of corporate good conduct and fulfil a function that no other institution can: we must remain vigilant that efforts to curb its 'excesses' do not damage its enormously valuable input. Arguably, without the press, corporate governance would not be the live issue it is today.

The annual report

The annual report plays an important role as a communications tool and, for many organisations, represents their main 'window on the world' for a wide range of audiences. Changes in the presentation and format of the annual report and the way the information is worded and structured seem to represent a positive trend.

Governmental bodies are beginning to see its potential as a catalyst for change. Recent proposals that companies should be forced to reveal in their annual report the average length of time before suppliers' invoices are paid is a case in point: another is the increased information as to directors' emoluments and their contract terms.

More responsible organisations are taking the opportunity to use the annual report to communicate their ethical position on a variety of issues to the outside world. Sainsbury's 1992 report, for instance, laudably devotes a great deal of space to setting out its policy with regard to:-

- suppliers;
- health and safety;
- urban regeneration and the community;
- employees and training;
- the environment.

While the annual report and accounts are, primarily, dealing with the historical financial position as at and up to the last accounting date, more opportunity should be taken to inform about current policies and future plans - going, we suggest, beyond the statutory requirements.

The communications audit

Internal communications are often wrongly seen as of secondary importance to the external. The communications audit is increasingly used to ensure that employee communications are satisfactory and effective. Corporate communications audits are now recognised as being an integral part of the business planning process, ensuring that communications activity works to assist in achieving business objectives. A professional communications audit does not look at a single element of the communications mix (such as advertising). It looks at the image projected by the organisation as a whole.

There are five key areas on which such an audit will need to focus to achieve its aims:-

- Scope and context: the audit must be flexible in examining the needs of all the organisation's audiences and in identifying the internal cultural barriers which inhibit the achievement of the business and the goods it markets;
- Monitoring and measuring: the audit must enable communications activity to become more measurable, defining targets and monitoring success;
- Setting objectives and parameters: the purpose of corporate communications activity is to further business objectives;
- Prioritizing resources: the audit should identify those activities, structures or mechanisms which are most effective in conveying the right messages to the most important audiences;
- Message identification and development: the audit must define what are the most important messages from a corporate perspective. It should examine the degree of credibility, plausibility and indeed interest in those messages by key internal and external audiences.

The institutional investor as a catalyst for change

The institutional investor is the most obvious catalyst for change because of the immense power institutional investors and their advisers can wield. Although UK institutions might sometimes find it in their own overall and long term interest to exert influence over company boards, in practice they have found their (potential) responsibilities too onerous to exert an active influence. They also tend to take a short term view (immediate dividend policy, potential for capitalising on gains to date) rather than conduct a campaign for increase in shareholder value.

The challenge still exists for management to create and foster a genuine dialogue with institutional shareholders, rather than just depend on the vagaries of the occasional lunch programme. Ironically, however, the reticence in the UK seems to come as much from the institutions themselves as from the companies. One is told privately, and with obvious embarrassment, that institutions do not want to give more 'unnecessary' management time to their investments; that they do not want to take on the additional legal responsibilities and liabilities that might arise from a quasi non-executive or shadow position; that the City as a whole is incapable of acting as a coherent body in this respect (or in its overall attitudes to major corporations) and that corporate management teams are best left to do 'the managing'. Ultimately, one is often told, shareholders hold the sanction of voting with their feet, but they demonstrably do not do so unless forcibly and forcefully led by the major shareholders i.e. the institutions. The City, and the institutions that comprise it, do not seem to be ready for the responsibility that goes with true ownership. Until that responsibility is accepted and acted upon, this catalyst for change will remain dormant.

In the meantime, several trends are already underway, each of which is positive within the scope of its own limitations:-

- investor relations programmes should and will become more widespread and more extensive;
- more discussions with major shareholders and City analysts will take place;
- the annual report will become more widely used as a 'shop window' for openness, and to demonstrate the company's adoption of good corporate governance principles, and (vitally) how far those principles are being followed in practice.

Until institutional shareholders are prepared to stand up and be counted, and have the courage to insist on the right lines of communication and consultation being established, until good corporate governance becomes an imposed requirement (with sanctions for non-observance) rather than Cadburyesque exhortation, the initiative for change will remain within corporations to do what they want, and not what they don't: and, of course, those corporations which are most in need of change and the penetrating gaze of an objective outsider will be those which are least likely to make progress.

While many of the most powerful participants in the corporate governance arena do not sufficiently want improvement to take place, matters will be allowed to carry on as they always have. As ever, the real losers will be the weaker interest bodies (the pensioners, suppliers and private investors) who will be the last to find out when things have gone wrong. If communication is not made more regular and more transparent, progress towards higher standards of corporate governance will not be made by those companies who most need it.

11 Corporate governance abroad and overseas influences and practices

This chapter seeks to discuss the extent to which corporate governance is a live issue in various overseas jurisdictions. By studying how the issue is being tackled elsewhere, and why in certain jurisdictions it is not perceived to be an issue at all, we gain a wider perspective on our own debate. Of particular interest and importance, is the project entitled 'Principles of Corporate Governance: Analysis and Recommendations' by the American Law Institute (ALI), and we devote a section of this chapter to a discussion of the ALI project (which is not included amongst the 'Relevant Published Statements' appended to Final Cadbury).

A comparative study cannot, however, universally be made in terms of a common background or culture. Varieties of approach and emphasis are not the only differences between countries. The starting point of the debate is often not the same. The unitary system of boards of directors within the United Kingdom is mirrored primarily in other common law countries. Civil law countries provide for a dual or two-tier board system (the most notable example being Germany). Thus the nature of the structure and indeed the matrix at the root of corporate governance vary widely, country by country. Further, the investor profile of foreign companies can also be very different For example the company's bankers in Germany are strong and active shareholders, both in their own right, and as proxy holders with strong voting power. The involvement of labour representatives in decision making (e.g. works councils in the Netherlands and the regime for co-determination in Germany) also reduce the influence and voting power of the shareholders.

Any discussion of corporate governance abroad must therefore begin with an analysis of the main relevant features of corporate legal structures abroad, in order to understand how far they respond to the issues of delegated accountability which are at the root of the debate. It will be particularly relevant to analyse the extent to which, and the manner in which, under foreign jurisdictions, directors are answerable to the general body of shareholders. This requires an analysis of directors' primary duties and establishing how far their performance is effectively monitored by or on behalf of shareholders. It is, likewise, instructive to evaluate the extent to which those directors who are not full time executives working for the company are involved in such sensitive issues as remuneration levels for the executives, and the format and contents of the company's accounts.

We must ask whether the strong, almost hands-on element of shareholder representation to be found in supervisory boards under the two-tier system solves many corporate governance issues at a stroke, or renders a debate on those issues an unnecessary and sterile diversion. But these questions must, in the UK context, be set against our domestic opposition to adopting a two-tier system (see the 1977 Report of the 'Bullock' Committee of Inquiry on Industrial Democracy) or anything that might be feared to approach having such a system (see our chapter 12 on Cadbury and the references there to opposition by UK industry on even having a number of NEDs on company boards as a matter of obligation).

Continental Europe

The two-tier system

The European corporate two-tier system consists of two layers of board structure. There is, as it were on top, the supervisory board or council (whose members may in some respects be considered to be the equivalent of our NEDs) and the management board (composed of senior executives in the company). A right of employee representation on the supervisory board is inherent in some jurisdictions.

Germany

In Germany, a two-tier system (with a supervisory board and a management board) is compulsory for almost all stock corporations ('Aktiengesellschaft' (AG)) and for such limited liability companies ('Gesellschaft mit beschränkter Haftung' (GmbH)) as have over 500 employees and are, consequently, subject to 'co-determination'.

For other (small and medium sized) German companies, the two-tier system is optional and seldom adopted. However such companies do often provide in their statutes for a so-called 'advisory board' ('Beirat'). The Beirat is much less formalised than a supervisory board, with more restricted powers and duties. There is no requirement for labour representation, and, in practice, such representation is seldom found.

The composition of the supervisory board for co-determination AGs and for co-determination GmbHs will be dependent upon how many employees work in the company: the more employees, the more labour representatives there will be on the supervisory board. Dependent on numbers of employees, between one third and one half of the supervisory board members will be labour representatives, with shareholders' representatives making up the balance of between two thirds and one half. This strong labour representation is not, of itself, a consequence of the German two-tier system: it is rather primarily a consequence of co-determination applying to the company in question, that application then being neatly accommodated within the two-tier system. It follows that companies not subject to co-determination (almost exclusively GmbHs) may have the two-tier system, but without labour representation.

The supervisory board's main functions are firstly to appoint and supervise the company's management, with powers to dismiss management, and secondly to report to shareholders' meetings as to the development of the company and the performance of management. Supervisory board members may not therefore also be members of the company's management board in order to avoid conflicts of interest and function. Those supervisory board members elected as labour representatives may be removed only according to the rules of the applicable Co-Determination Act. Supervisory board members elected as shareholders' representatives are likely to be representatives of banks, of local communities, executives of other companies, independent lawyers or accountants, and the local 'great and good'. They may be removed by majority resolution of shareholders. Otherwise, in serious cases, the supervisory board itself may apply to the court to remove a supervisory board member.

The management board ('Vorstand' or 'Geschäftsführung') will consist of one or more members, the number and their designated general tasks (e.g. as labour director) depending on the type of company, the size of its nominal share capital, and the number of its employees. The management board is responsible for the day to day business of the company, and for financial accountability.

In a GmbH, the adoption of the annual accounts and the declaration of dividends are matters for the shareholders to vote on. The management board will prepare the annual accounts for submission to shareholders, and will decide whether or not to make provision for a dividend.

In an AG, the management board is responsible for the preparation of the annual accounts which are to be adopted by the supervisory board and the management board.

Shareholders cannot change the annual accounts of an AG once they have been adopted by the management board and the supervisory board. Thenceforth, with respect to the amount of the dividend, shareholders will be bound by the proposed profit distribution as shown in the (approved) annual accounts.

The voting strength of shareholders in German Stock Exchange listed companies is often found to lie in the hands of their bankers. This is not only because, as we have seen, German banks are often themselves equity investors in their corporate customers, but even more significantly as a result of the practice of private and institutional shareholders granting permanent voting proxies to bankers who will, usually, co-operate with each other as to the use of their own and their proxy votes.

The extent of shareholders' influence in German quoted companies is currently the subject of frequent debate. Whilst, in theory, shareholders can exercise their voting rights in general meetings and thereby influence the composition and identity of the shareholders' representatives on the supervisory board, in practice shareholders' influence is quite small. This is due, in part, to this practice of granting proxies to the bankers who routinely send to their customers proxy forms for completion and signature. Thus, rights to speak, question and vote at general meetings are ceded by individual shareholders to their bankers.

Further, the low level of shareholders' influence is due to the fact that the shareholders may only vote on basic and structural issues, and not on decisions as to the day to day business. In particular, they have no right directly to interfere with, or direct, the members of the management board, who are responsible for their own decisions. Whilst up to one half of the members of the supervisory board may be labour representatives, the chairman, who is nominated by the shareholders, always has the casting vote.

A further reason for the low level of shareholders' influence is that the shareholders have **no vote at all** on the composition and identity of up to one half of the members of the supervisory board, namely the labour representatives. Labour representatives on the supervisory board are required to behave and act responsibly in the interests of the broad outlook of the company as a whole, rather than, narrowly, only in the interest of employees. This requirement is not, however, as comforting as it might sound, since labour representatives do not usually view their own position as likely to place them in a situation of conflict of interest. Typically, in their opinion, the interests of the employees can be regarded as coinciding with the interests of the company. Whilst this may, generally, be the case in times of full employment, Germany, post unification, does not currently enjoy either the same industrial strength or full employment as in the past.

The Netherlands

The Netherlands has a similar basic two-tier structure, with a supervisory board and a management board, applicable to both public companies ('NVs') and private companies ('BVs'), although this structure is only compulsory for 'large' corporations. A corporation can voluntarily adopt the status of being 'large' (often as a result of negotiations with unions or works councils) even if it does not fall within the statutory definitions for being 'large'.

The supervisory board of a 'large' corporation must consist of at least three individuals (not corporations) and they cannot also serve on the management board. They are usually appointed for a four year term by the existing supervisory directors themselves, albeit by following a procedure which involves notifying shareholders, the management board and the works council of an anticipated vacancy. Subject to that procedure, however, the supervisory board can be seen as self-perpetuating.

The Dutch supervisory board for large companies has three main functions:-

- election and dismissal of the management board;
- adoption of the annual accounts; and
- approval of specified important decisions (e.g. issuing shares, acquisitions and major investments), and applying for a Stock Exchange listing,

some of which might be expected to fall within the matters reserved for the shareholders in other jurisdictions.

In smaller (i.e. not large) companies (which are numerically far more prevalent), the duties of the supervisory board are to oversee the policy of the management board and its general business activities, and to advise the management board. In the performance of its duties, the supervisory board has to act in the general interest of the company, but does not have to report to meetings of shareholders. It provides the checks and balances on management activities, rather than supervises them. The two functions of supervision and management are regarded as separate. Supervisory board members will normally be independent experts (commercial, legal, tax, etc), representatives of family shareholders or of joint venture partners, or be representatives of government or of the banks.

The supervisory board of large companies must be 'suitably composed'. Thus a (Dutch) labour representative should be appointed to the supervisory board, especially where the sole shareholder is a foreign company and the majority of the board consists only of representatives who are not familiar with the Dutch social and economic situation. The labour representative has to act in accordance with the general interests of the company, and not only the interests of the labour force. Conflicts of interest do not often rise to the surface, although they may swim around not far below it.

In the Netherlands, the shareholders are not the supreme authority within the corporation. Particularly in 'large' corporations, they have limited powers - deliberately so because with the mandatory two-tier system alongside these limited shareholder powers, the power of the employee-based works council is increased. Granting shareholders' voting proxies to banks is rare. Banks prefer a nominee on the supervisory board, rather than holding shareholders' proxies at general meetings. In the context of shareholders' limited powers, this is perhaps understandable.

The management board is responsible for the management of the company, with collective powers and responsibilities. It may consist of some directors who are corporations, but it does not have power to fill its own vacancies. Managing directors are elected by the supervisory board in large companies, usually for an indefinite period - but otherwise by the shareholders. The management board is responsible for preparing the annual accounts and an annual report. Its role is an independent one, and it is not subordinated to either the shareholders or to the supervisory board, although supervisory board approval must be obtained in large companies prior to the company undertaking major changes (e.g. stock issues) or major acquisitions or joint ventures.

France

We turn now to consider the position in France. All our research into the position in the Republic points, in all fields of corporate governance and corporate management, to the existence, power and overwhelming influence of an 'élite'. Perhaps, in the United Kingdom of Great Britain and Northern Ireland, we would have referred to such an élite as 'the old school tie', but such a thing still exists strongly in the Republic of France. The existence and power of such an élite pervades the entire managerial system in France and is probably one of its major underlying features. Power and influence are reciprocally given and accorded to those who have a close and long-standing relationship, going back to their days together at school, college, university and polytechnics. This relationship subsists between top level civil servants and top management of leading companies and, in turn, has a strong influence on the economic life in France.

In France, since 1966, the option of a two-tier system for the Société Anonyme (limited company 'SA') has been optional. The traditional system however remains a unitary one. According to a 1975 EEC Green Paper:-

> only a small proportion of companies have adopted this [two-tier] structure and many of those who originally adopted it have reverted to the old classical system.

The Green Paper went on to say:-

> the reason for these developments appears to be that friction and
> conflict have occurred in a significant proportion of dualist companies
> as a result of the supervisory councils having difficulty in confining
> themselves to control, and trespassing on management territory. It has
> often been difficult to resolve these conflicts, because only the general
> assembly of shareholders has the power to remove the management
> committee, which deprives the supervisory council of an important
> means of coercion.

One of the reasons put forward for the introduction of a two-tier system in
France was the possibility thus afforded for the two boards to split between them
the powers and responsibilities, and also to increase the number of board seats
at supervisory and management board level. This reason is still not perceived
as an adequate or sufficient reason for the two-tier system to be accepted or
widely adopted in France. It is still felt that efficiency, simplicity and secrecy
are best catered for in a system where almost all the powers to manage are
concentrated in the hands of one person, namely the Président Directeur
Générale (PDG) to whom we will refer later.

The option in France of having a two-tier system involves the management of
the company being shared between a management board ('directoire') and a
supervisory board ('conseil de surveillance'). The functions of the supervisory
board are to oversee what the management board has done and is planning to do,
receiving a report from the management board at least every three months.
Additionally, a company's statutes can specify a range of substantial or
constitutional matters on which the supervisory board has to be consulted in
advance and its authorisation obtained before the management board can
proceed. The supervisory board has to present its own comments to shareholders
on the report of the management board and on the company's annual accounts.
The supervisory board determines who shall be chairman of the management
board and fixes the levels of remuneration of the management board members.

The members of the supervisory board (minimum three, maximum twelve) are
appointed by the shareholders; they must themselves be shareholders, therefore
board members can be corporations: they are paid nominal fees plus expenses
only, and generally neither employees nor members of the management board
are eligible for appointments to the supervisory board. The members of the
supervisory board may be dismissed for any reason and at any time by resolution
at a shareholders' general meeting.

The members of the management board may (and usually will) be full time executive employees of the company, and they can be dismissed by shareholders' meetings but **only** on a proposal submitted by the supervisory board. Without such a proposal, the shareholders themselves have no powers of dismissal. There must be a minimum of two board members (one for small companies) and there is a maximum of five (seven if the company's shares are listed on the Stock Exchange).

SAs which do not adopt the two-tier board system must have a board of directors ('conseil d'administration') of between three and twelve members (administrateurs) who may be individuals or companies, but who must be shareholders of the company. All directors must be appointed by resolution of a general meeting of shareholders for terms of not more than six years. Any director may be removed from office for any reason by resolution of a general meeting. An employee of the company may be appointed a director only if his contract of employment was entered into at least two years before his appointment, but employees may not hold more than one third of the total number of directorships (i.e. effectively, at least two thirds must be NEDs). Directors must hold a number of qualification shares which form a fund which may be resorted to in order to compensate the company for breaches of duty by any of the directors. Directors may now be remunerated only by fees. The previous right of directors to a share of the company's profits ('tantième') was abolished in 1975.

The board of directors, nominally, has 'full power to act in all circumstances in the name of a company ... within the limits of its objects and subject to the powers conferred by law on the general meeting of shareholders'. However, the directors must elect one of their number to be the chairman/managing director (PDG) who 'undertakes on his own responsibility the general direction of the company'. Subject to the powers of the general meeting conferred by law and the limits imposed by the company's objects, he is vested with full power to act in all circumstances in the name of the company'. This, inevitably and deliberately, places enormous power into the hands of the PDG. For an SA with the traditional structure of a board of directors and a PDG, which is by far the most common, the PDG can, if he so wishes, exercise very extensive powers. The main historical reason for this is that under French corporate law, the powers of the PDG are derived from general legal provisions, rather than dependent upon delegated powers being passed down to the PDG by the board of directors. Rather, the PDG is recognised as holding all management powers by virtue of his appointment as such. The PDG may, however, be dismissed at any time for any reason and without indemnity. Any contractual provision intended to or resulting in limitations to this right of dismissal in the hands of the shareholders will be deemed to be null and void. However, this is largely theoretical, because the élitist system will ensure, almost inevitably, due protection being accorded to the PDG, as a fellow member of the élite.

As a consequence of the power and position of the PDG, the powers of shareholders to influence, intervene and use their voting rights effectively, are limited. Thus the board's effective functions are reduced to calling meetings of shareholders and presenting the directors' annual report, consenting to share transfers where this is necessary, approving contracts in which directors are interested and approving the creation of mortgages over the company's property and the giving of guarantees by it.

There is no statutory right of employees to appoint labour representatives onto the management board or the supervisory board, but if an SA employs more than 50 persons it must establish a works council ('comité d'entreprise') whose members are elected by the employees. The works council may send two of its members as observers to meetings of the management board and of the supervisory board, but they cannot vote. Further, it is common practice amongst boards of French companies who do have such a works council to have preliminary board meetings, without the representatives of the works council being in attendance, during which sensitive issues can be examined and effectively determined in the absence of the works council representatives.

The traditional corporate pressure groups on the part of employees used to be the 'syndicats' or trades unions. However, their influence and power has considerably reduced over the past years, partially due to significant labour conflicts arising, which led to the growth of so-called 'co-ordinations'. These acted independently of the unions and represented the claims and demands of the employees.

There is legal provision, in privately controlled companies, for directors to be appointed with power to represent employees working in the business. This has become compulsory in certain state owned companies, but is not common.

At the annual general meeting, it is the function of the shareholders to approve the annual accounts and the reports of the management board, supervisory board and of the auditors, to declare dividends and to appoint members of the management and supervisory boards, and to appoint the auditors.

The directors have the obligation to prepare annual accounts comprising an inventory, trading account, profit and loss account and balance sheet, and submit them to the auditors for examination and report. The accounts and the auditors report, together with the reports of the board of directors and committee of supervision are then laid before the annual meeting of shareholders for approval.

The need for NEDs, audit committees or remuneration committees is not apparent in France, and there does not seem to be any pressure for their introduction, even on a voluntary basis. The adoption of good corporate governance practices, as understood in the UK and America, is not a topic of much relevance in France.

As to the issue of accountability to the general body of shareholders, in particular with Stock Exchange listed companies, a great effort has been made in France to improve the access of the public at large to data relating to companies. However, recent and major cases relating to insider dealing offences shed a negative and adverse light on the overall situation particularly where there was an element of state ownership. The state could deal in the market and take advantage of market opportunities without incurring sanctions.

Spain

Spain comes close to France on the structural spectrum of corporate governance. Sociedades Anonimas (limited companies) are regulated by new legislation passed in 1989 to adapt Spanish company law to the EEC Directives. Management of a company can be granted to one sole administrator or to several persons. If a sole administrator is appointed to represent the company, he is primarily and personally liable so far as the company, the shareholders and third parties are concerned. The administrator does not have to hold any shares in the company. Plurality of administrators does not imply the existence of a board of directors. The 1989 Companies Act requires the creation of a board of directors only when more than two administrators are appointed and they are mandated to exercise their powers together.

The alternative, namely the board of directors ('consejo de administracion') is also appointed by the general meeting of shareholders.

The board of directors can delegate its functions, unless precluded by the statutes of the company, to a managing director ('consejo delegado'), who must be a member of the board. He can either be vested with all the powers and responsibilities of the board, or only with those which the board has decided to grant him. The board can also delegate its functions to an executive committee ('comision ejecutiva'), made up of a reduced number of the directors, by an express decision at a board meeting, in which the responsibilities of the executive committee are defined. This practice is particularly prevalent in corporations which have a large numbers of directors - mainly banks. Any permanent delegation, either to an individual or an executive committee, requires a two thirds majority from the board; it also has to be registered at the Mercantile Registry.

Remuneration of the directors and their period of appointment are not covered in detail by the Spanish Companies Act. The Act limits only the extent of any profit sharing element, making it subject first to the maintenance of legal and statutory reserves, and secondly to the payment of a dividend of at least 4% of paid-up share capital to shareholders. As to the period of appointment, any applicable limitations will be laid down in the statutes of the company, provided the period does not exceed five years. However there is no restriction on the number of times a board member can be re-elected by a general meeting of shareholders. Directors' remuneration has to be disclosed in the company's annual report, which has to be filed at the Mercantile Registry, and which is thus open to public inspection.

The Spanish Companies Act sets out a certain number of corporate functions and decisions which cannot be exercised by the board of directors. These issues are to be decided by the general meeting of shareholders, and they include principally:-

● the appointment and removal of members of the board of directors;
● dissolution, winding up or divestment of a company;
● approval of the annual accounts and the declaration of annual dividends;
● modification of the statutes of the company;
● increases or reductions in company capital.

Proxy voting by banks on behalf of their customers is unusual in Spain.

The position in Spain with regard to auditors is interesting. In order to protect their independence, and to avoid the relationship between the company and the auditors becoming too close, the 1989 Act limits to nine the number of consecutive accounting periods that can be audited by the same firm. Once that maximum has been reached, at least three accounting periods must elapse before the firm can be reappointed. However, once appointed, the company cannot change its auditors without 'just cause'.

A varied and nationalistic approach in Europe

We have limited our discussion on the varied corporate and structural systems in Continental Europe to Germany, the Netherlands, France and Spain only, because those countries seem to us to present the most interesting range of approaches from a corporate governance standpoint. We have in particular noted:-

● in Germany, the voting strength of banks and the power, through representation on the supervisory board, of the labour force for co-determination companies;

- in the Netherlands, the powers of the labour force through works councils and that the shareholders are not the supreme or ultimate authority for corporate influence;
- in France, the reluctance to use the optional two-tier system, the strength of concentration of power in the PDG, supported by the 'élite' and the consequential lack of effective shareholder influence and power;
- in Spain, the mandatory provisions for the periodical change of auditor.

Each seems content with its own system, built up over the years and influenced by its own history. The adoption of what we, in the UK, are beginning to accept as proper requirements for improved corporate governance not only fails to fit comfortably with national corporate structures, it also seems an irrelevance. Will it ever be thus?

With such a varied range of corporate structures, philosophies, national characteristics and powers, respectively, of management and shareholders, the UK providing yet further variations, it is hardly surprising that the EC company law directives (which are framed to apply only to public companies and remain at the draft stage) followed the French system by laying down two alternatives models for corporate management.

One model is a two-tier system under which the company is to have a management board running its day to day affairs, supervised by a supervisory board, without the same person being allowed to be a member of both boards, but with the supervisory board having the power to dismiss the management board.

Alternatively, there is the one tier model, which involves one board namely an administrative board, governing the company and its affairs and with management being delegated to executive members of that board.

The current draft directive also sets out three alternative schemes for employee participation, these, in decreasing order of labour representative power, being as follows:-

- a system under which there is employee participation in the appointment of the members of the supervisory board;
- a system under which the employee participation is through a body representing employees of the company;
- an alternative third system where employee participation is regulated through collective agreements between the company and the organisations representing the employees.

The strength and individuality of any nation state is a product of its own history and culture. In Europe, the history and culture of each does not merely differ one to the other, and thus present contrasting background to the structures, systems and 'mores' which each has developed and finds acceptable. They have also grown through past conflicts - nation with nation. No one should compel or exhort national change for the sake of change, or for the sake of an artificial (therefore inevitably unsuccessful) imposed uniformity. In Europe, our structures for and concepts of corporate governance vary, as has been seen, very widely indeed. It would be a lamentable example of empirical and arrogant self-satisfaction for any nation to seek to impose its own systems on its neighbours, even motivated by the best of peaceful and federal objectives. It would, however, be shameful not to share our experiences and problems with our friends, and tell them of the potential solutions we have devised.

National structures and systems within Europe will remain at variance, one with the other, and so it should be.

United States of America

America, as is well known, has a federal legal system. The structure of the corporate laws affecting the corporation itself is largely legislated for by State laws. Federal laws, of applicability throughout all the States, function primarily, for our purposes, as an adjunct to stock market status.

The (Federal) Investment Company Act of 1940 includes in its requirements that 60% of the directors are unrelated to the advisor. It authorises the Securities and Exchange Commission (SEC) to remove directors and officers involved in misconduct.

Management and corporate structures adopted are not generally matters of compliance with legal requirements. State corporation laws typically stipulate that corporations are to be managed by their boards of directors, but otherwise say very little about management structures.

American boards of directors of public and major corporations are typically comprised primarily of 'outside directors' who are not employees of the corporation, with some 'inside' directors, namely 'officers' of the corporation such as the president, the chief executive officer and possibly a number of senior vice-presidents. So models of the organs of corporate governance in the US have evolved, not been prescribed by law.

There is a growing trend towards the inclusion of more 'outside' directors, namely those who are not employed full-time by the company. The role of these 'disinterested' directors is also increasing. The SEC believes (and US Stock

Exchanges require) that certain board duties may only be undertaken by outside directors. For example, SEC rules provide that only outside directors may sit on the audit committee of the board. This requirement is intended to ensure that inside directors do not have too strong an influence upon the financial activities of the board or upon the work of the independent auditor.

In the US, the board of directors is selected by the shareholders at a shareholders meeting. The board's primary mandate, in general, is to select the 'officers' (i.e. executive management) who will run the corporation, and to establish corporate policy. Unlike the situation in the United Kingdom, US directors cannot bind the corporation: this can only be done by the authorised officers. Conversely, officers are generally not authorised to make strategic or policy decisions for the corporation. Rather, the officers will make a proposal for a strategic or policy initiative and present it to the board for consideration. The board may then accept the proposal by resolution, or reject it.

Whilst the system of having a board consisting mainly of NEDs and having executive officers of the corporation equates neither to the two-tier system in Continental Europe nor to the UK unitary system, it embraces elements of each.

Under US law, the directors have a fiduciary duty to the people who elected them, namely the shareholders. In recent years, there has been a spate of suits against directors and officers for a breach of that duty. Consequently, it has become more and more difficult to find people to sit on boards of directors.

Dramatic developments occurred during 1992 in the United States.

Firstly the boards of directors of two of its most famous and widely held corporations, International Business Machines and General Motors, each not only fired their chief executive officers but also took far more active roles in the business affairs of their companies. In doing so, they reflected a variety of new and general pressures on boards of directors, pressures which also led the boards of many other prominent but lesser known companies to take a far more involved role in their companies' affairs.

What are the pressures that moved boards to take such strong and, for many companies, unprecedented actions? First, for some years now the SEC has maintained that the boards of
public companies have tended to be too passive and too close to management. The SEC argues that this tendency has resulted in failure adequately to oversee worrying practices in such areas as takeover protection (e.g. the adoption of poison pills), executive compensation, creative accounting and inadequate disclosure.

Also in 1992, the SEC took two major concrete steps to combat these perceived trends. First, in new rules largely devoted to expanding disclosure of executive compensation and perquisites, the SEC required the compensation committee of a company's board of directors to state explicitly, in its annual proxy statement, the basis for its decisions about executive compensation levels and practices. Secondly, responding specifically to institutional shareholders, the SEC also ordered a significant deregulation of the proxy process, giving shareholders a new (and, historically, extraordinary) freedom publicly to raise issues regarding listed companies, including but not confined to those issues put to a vote of shareholders, without prior clearance by the SEC.

These SEC moves responded to the rise of institutional shareholder activism. Over one half of all equities of publicly owned American companies are now owned by 'institutional investors', including pension funds (both public and private), endowments and foundations, and mutual funds and other pooled investment vehicles. These long sleeping giants had followed the simple rule of 'vote yes or sell'. However, these organisations now collectively and individually express directly to management their frustration over inadequate corporate performance, seek removal of barriers to takeovers (shareholder rights plans, poison pill devices, classified boards, executive severance agreements, and others) and aim to separate the functions and offices of the chairman of the board and the chief executive officer. In such situations as Sears Roebuck and US Steel, institutional shareholders have been prominent and successful in persuading boards and management to restructure those companies with major divestitures.

A further threat that confronts boards of directors is the increasing possibility of actual liability to shareholders for failure adequately to oversee the activities of their companies. Although no court decisions have, as yet, resulted in significant damages being awarded against directors, the concern for this liability has grown pervasive, and, with it, corresponding growth in the use of directors' and officers' liability insurance policies.

Another reaction to all these pressures at a number of companies has been for the board to retain its own, separate and independent law counsel to advise it on its particular responsibility for the affairs of the company. In some situations where chief executives have been replaced at the instigation of outside directors, notably at General Motors and Goodyear Tire and Rubber, press reports have suggested that advice from independent outside counsel has played a major role in encouraging the board to take action.

Looking ahead, it is clear that the new more involved boards of directors of American public companies are probably here to stay. All the elements which led to this change (SEC concern with the role and composition of boards, institutional shareholders demanding both results and open governance structures, and the threat of liability for failure to exercise effective board authority) are growing more prominent, not less so. Their effects continue to be visible and to motivate boards of directors throughout the entire US corporate community.

The ALI project

In the opening paragraphs of this chapter, we referred to this project which provides perhaps the best, widest ranging and most thought provoking analysis and recommendations in the field of corporate governance to us in the UK. The fact that the ALI deals with the issue from an American standpoint in no way reduces the impact of much of the ALI's work in the context of the UK debate on the issue.

The ALI project was started in 1982, and thus anticipated both the trends which built up to the dramatic developments in 1992 to which we have already referred and also the growing pressure for improvement and change in the UK for which momentum grew through the 1980s, leading to the setting up of the Cadbury Committee.

The ALI project has produced a mammoth Draft Report, now over 1,000 pages in length. Each Recommendation has appended to it a learned comment and analysis of its derivation or novelty.

In his foreword to the 'Proposed Final Draft' of March 31, 1992, Mr Geoffrey C Hazard Jr, Director of the ALI, appended 'a special note of appreciation' to Mr Roswell B Perkins, President of the ALI. We, too, acknowledge his help to us and his contributions and support in the compilation of this book.

In his foreword, Mr Hazard goes to the root of corporate governance as a 'complex subject that has many controversial aspects' and, in response to some of the critical comments that have been directed to the project, says this:-

> Corporate governance involves the general management of substantial enterprises. The general management of a substantial enterprise is a complex and dynamic process requiring continual practical responses by necessarily fallible agents exercising power and authority under conditions that are usually subject to unremitting change and often great uncertainty. The law, whatever its subject, requires definite legal premises for its administration. The law of corporate governance therefore entails making legally definitive prescriptions that must be applied to circumstances that have to be fixed after the fact by the procedural and evidentiary law. Moreover, both corporate governance and the judicial administration of corporate law entail heavy responsibilities to society at large.

... The Principles [of corporate governance] have also sought to define the accommodations between strongly held but often competing values widely shared in our political culture: on the one hand, freedom of enterprise; on the other, accountability under the law.

The Report, comprising the ALI's 'Analysis and Recommendations', is set out in seven parts as follows:-

- Definitions;
- The objective and conduct of the corporation;
- Corporate structure: Functions and powers of directors and officers; audit committee in large publicly held corporations;
- Recommendations of corporate practice concerning the board and the principal oversight committee;
- Duty of care and the business judgment rule;
- Duty of fair dealing;
- Role of directors and shareholders in transactions in control and tender offers;
- Remedies.

We propose, here, to focus on but a small extract of the Report, namely those Recommendations which seem to be particularly apposite and relevant to us in the UK in our quest for improved standards of corporate governance.

Paragraph 2.01 of ALI sets out a summary of 'The objective and conduct of the corporation'. It says that:-

A corporation should have as its objective the conduct of business activities with a view to enhancing corporate profit and shareholder gain.

It goes on to say that even if corporate profit and shareholder gain are not thereby enhanced, the corporation, in the conduct of its business, is obliged to act within the boundaries set by law, may take into account ethical considerations that are reasonably regarded as appropriate to the responsible conduct of business, and may devote a reasonable amount of resources to public welfare, humanitarian, educational and philanthropic purposes.

The adoption of such objectives would readily fall within the corporate philosophy of most UK companies. If the objectives were clearly set out, perhaps in the company's report and accounts, shareholders would have a clearer picture of what the directors consider to be their mandate.

When introducing the proposed structure of the corporation, ALI states that its recommendations 'reflect two highly important social needs regarding such [publicly held] corporations':-

> One is the need to permit a corporation to be highly flexible in structuring its operational management. The other is the need for processes that ensure managerial accountability to shareholders for accomplishing the objective of the corporation.

ALI goes on to say:-

> Broadly speaking, three kinds of corporate and social institutions contribute towards satisfying the need for managerial accountability: direct review by the body of shareholders; the discipline of the product and capital markets and of tender offers; and oversight of management by the board of directors and its committees.

Again, this philosophy and these social needs have direct relevance to us in the UK.

The emphasis on the role of the capital markets (i.e., here, the Stock Exchange) echoes our approach, as does also a strengthening of shareholder activism and the emphasis on the function of the board of directors being 'oversight' rather than direct involvement in management. This latter point is of particular relevance to any distinction that may be introduced into English law as to the separate and distinct functions of non-executive directors, and provides a useful precedent for definition.

3.02 of ALI sets out recommendations on the functions and powers of the (mostly non-executive) board of directors in America.

3.02 is worthy of quotation in its entirety. It says:-

> Except as otherwise provided by statute:
>
> (a) the board of directors of a publicly held corporation should perform the following functions:
>
>   (1) select, regularly evaluate, fix the compensation of, and, where appropriate, replace the principal senior executives;

      (2)   oversee the conduct of the corporation's business to evaluate whether the business is being properly managed;

      (3)   review and, where appropriate, approve the corporation's financial objectives and major corporate plans and actions;

      (4)   review and, where appropriate, approve major changes in, and determinations of other major questions of choice respecting, the appropriate auditing and accounting principles and practices to be used in the preparation of the corporation's financial statements;

      (5)   perform such other functions as are prescribed by law, or assigned to the board under a standard of the corporation;

(b)   a board of directors also has power to:-

      (1)   initiate and adopt corporate plans, commitments and actions;

      (2)   initiate and adopt changes in accounting principles and practices;

      (3)   provide advice and counsel to the principal senior executives;

      (4)   instruct any committee, principal senior executive or other officer, and review the actions of any committee, principal senior executive or other officer;

      (5)   make recommendations to shareholders;

      (6)   manage the business of the corporation;

      (7)   act as to all other corporate matters not requiring shareholder approval;

(c)   Subject to the board's ultimate responsibility for oversight ... the board may delegate to its committees authority to perform any of its functions and exercise any of its powers.

There is no better summary of the role and functions and powers of boards of directors. The emphasis is on manpower, evaluation, business oversight and review, determining accounting principles and practices, initiating and adopting corporate plans and strategies. The power to delegate is, realistically, vital (again, contrast with Cadbury's CBP 1.1, recommending that the board should "retain full and effective control over the company' as well as 'monitor the executive management'). The ALI precedent is wholly realistic; more so than Gallery.

The above list of functions and powers of the board of directors is supplemented, in ALI, by sections dealing with directors' informational rights, directors' rights to retain outside experts, directors' rights of reliance on directors, officers, employees, experts and other persons, and on committees of the board, with detailed provisions that provide that:-

> ...a director or officer who makes a business judgment in good faith fulfils the duty [of care] ... if the director or officer:
>
> (1)   is not interested in the subject of the business judgment;
>
> (2)   is informed with respect to the subject of the business judgment to the extent the director or officer reasonably believes to be appropriate under the circumstances; and
>
> (3)   rationally believes that the business judgment is in the best interests of the corporation.

The business judgment rule forms an important part of American jurisprudence, so far as duties of directors are concerned. Of the business judgment rule, the ALI project says this:-

> The basic policy underpinning the business judgment rule is that corporate law should encourage, and afford broad protection to, informed business judgments (whether subsequent events prove the judgments right or wrong) in order to stimulate risk taking, innovation and other creative entrepreneurial activities. Shareholders, with expectations of greater profit, accept the risk that an informed business decision - honestly undertaken and rationally believed to be in the best interests of the corporation - may not be vindicated by subsequent success. The special protection afforded business judgments is also

based on a desire to limit litigation and judicial intrusiveness with respect to private sector business decision making.

Many pages are devoted by ALI to the business judgment rule. It serves as a qualification to the directors' duty of care against the background of the risk of shareholder derivative actions against directors for alleged misfeasance. Many more pages (indeed almost one half of the ALI report) are devoted to remedies (e.g. by way of class or derivative actions) against directors.

Such actions are, as yet, unknown - or at least uncommon - in the common law system of the UK. No director here relishes the prospect of a transatlantic invasion of such law suits. The type of shareholder activism we have advocated in support of better practices of corporate governance should not be read as encouragement to litigate. But an understanding of the business judgment rule, and its judicial adoption here, would be both appropriate and welcome.

There is much to learn from the ALI, and gratefully to be borrowed from its report.

12 The work of the Cadbury Committee

The work of the Cadbury Committee on The Financial Aspects of Corporate Governance sought to define best practice. How well did it achieve its objective? What can we learn from its work, and from press and public comment about good corporate governance? Cadbury acts as a catalyst - a detailed critique of how far Cadbury felt able to go, and where it fell short assists in arriving at an understanding of current expectations and clarifies where improvements are still required.

The Cadbury Committee was set up in the spring of 1991 by the Financial Reporting Council, the accountancy profession and the London Stock Exchange to examine 'the financial aspects of corporate governance'. It had become clear that there was no uniformly applied system and framework by which companies are run in this country, and the sponsors were concerned at 'the perceived low level of confidence both in financial reporting and in the ability of auditors to provide the safeguards which the users of company reports sought and expected' (Introduction to Draft Report 2.1). Concern was also expressed about 'the absence of a clear framework for ensuring that Directors kept under review the controls in their business, together with the looseness of accounting standards and competitive pressures both on companies and on auditors which made it difficult for auditors to stand up to demanding boards' (ibid.).

Cadbury's terms of reference

The Committee's terms of reference were as follows:-

To consider the following issues in relation to financial reporting and accountability and to make recommendations on good practice:-

(i) the responsibilities of executive and non-executive directors for reviewing and reporting on performance to shareholders and other financially interested parties; and the frequency, clarity and form in which information should be provided;

(ii) the case for audit committees of the board, including their composition and role;

(iii) the principal responsibilities of auditors and the extent and value of the audit;

(iv) the links between shareholders, board and auditors
(v)   any other relevant matters.

The Draft Report

The Draft Report was published on 27 May 1992, and public comment was invited. The authors of this book responded to the invitation and submitted their own commentary to the Committee; many of the views expressed in that commentary are implicit in this chapter.

Cadbury was at pains to emphasise that the bulk of its recommendations should be taken as representing current best practice, rather than as attempting to impose fresh and more effectively radical solutions. We believe that it was in this reluctance to break new ground that the clue for the perceived inadequacies of Cadbury might be found to lie. The Committee thought it could say (Draft Cadbury 1.6) 'The basic system of corporate governance in the United Kingdom is sound'. It however mentioned a 'low level of confidence'. The contrast between these two statements is remarkable.

This all took place against a background of a small number of spectacular company failures (*Polly Peck, Maxwell, inter alia*). These gained the widest publicity and brought the whole subject of corporate governance prominently before the eye of many sections of the public. The controversial salary increases of some top directors might be said to have further jaundiced public opinion.

Corporate governance had suddenly become a very fashionable topic, and searching questions were being asked. Those asking the questions were going to expect more than generalised and vague statements about 'openness', 'integrity' and 'accountability' (concepts that feature strongly in Cadbury). They looked to Cadbury for a clear and unambiguous show of teeth, an acknowledgment that all in the corporate garden was not lovely. They wanted a firm set of recommendations to ensure that future inadequacies of governance would be strictly punished, and that appropriate sanctions would be imposed.

As a result of our work on this book we had, for many months before the publication of the Draft Report, been giving a great deal of thought to our own approach to the subject. We were pleased to see that some of our ideas and suggestions were echoed in the Draft Report which contains much material with which we agree, and which we welcome and endorse. This will be evident if this book is read, as it were, alongside Cadbury. Nevertheless we are not alone in having concluded that Cadbury lacks the essential elements of 'stick and carrot' to encourage achievement of the unarguable goal **which is compliance with the best principles of corporate governance**, clearly and enforceably enunciated.

At the heart of Cadbury lay 'The Code of Best Practice' (CBP), which they say is 'designed to achieve the necessary high standards of corporate behaviour'. The first mistake the Committee made, in our opinion, was to make the CBP theoretically voluntary. This was apparently done quite deliberately so as to avoid 'a greater reliance on regulation'. This also perhaps justified the unenforceable vagueness inherent in the CBP.

The CBP is directed 'to the boards of directors of all listed companies registered in the UK', but there is an encouragement that as many other companies as possible aim at meeting its requirements.

Cadbury suggests that the arguments for adhering to the CBP are twofold:-

(i)   'A clear understanding of responsibilities and an open approach to the way in which they have been discharged will assist boards of directors in framing and winning support for their strategies'. It will also, they say, assist in the efficient operation of capital markets and increase confidence in boards, auditors and financial reporting and hence the general level of confidence in business.

(ii)   If standards of financial reporting and of business conduct more generally are not seen to be raised, a greater reliance on regulation may be inevitable.

In Draft Cadbury 3.7 there was a welcome glint of teeth: 'We recommend that listed companies reporting in respect of years ending on or after 31 December 1992 should state in the report and accounts whether they comply with the Code and identify and give reasons for any areas of non-compliance. The London Stock Exchange intends to require such a statement as one of its continuing listing obligations.' The Stock Exchange has indeed after Final Cadbury imposed such a requirement (see, further, chapter 13).

The role of the Stock Exchange is vital as a monitor in a non-legislative system, but we would suggest a different and firmer approach, to be added to Section 5 of the Yellow Book as part of the continuing obligations, and to be adopted for new listings, so that eligibility for such a listing would be linked, additionally in the future, to the applicant company having adhered to our clear and mandatory Code of Practice (see chapter 13 and appendix A) prior to listing.

The Cadbury Code of Best Practice

Examination of Cadbury's CBP reveals a commendably brief document. It deals with four different topics, namely the board of directors, the non-executive directors, controls and reporting. So far as it goes it is (no doubt) a genuine attempt but, in our view it does not go nearly far enough. There are too many unrealistic requirements and pious hopes, and too much naive confidence. There are holes through which coaches and horses could and no doubt will be driven.

Our Code of Practice in appendix A, explained and discussed in chapter 13, tries to close most of these holes without inhibiting enterprise and directorial dynamism. By identifying the CBP's shortcomings here, we explain the foundations of our own Code.

Boards of directors

An example of the lack of realism (a lack notably absent in America - see chapter 11) is to be found in 1.1 of the Cadbury CBP:-

> The board must meet regularly, retain full and effective control over the company and monitor the executive management.

We agree that the board should meet regularly, but the remainder of the passage quoted ignores the inherent right of delegation which boards of directors have, and somehow requires the board's control over the company and its executive management to be 'full and effective'. We question what 'full and effective control' any of the boards of FTSE 100 companies would pretend to have, in practice.

Certainly there should be systems for monitoring and for financial and business control, but for it to be pretended that the board can, without delegation, 'retain' full and effective control over the company is quite unrealistic.

Paragraphs 1.2 and 1.3 of the CBP are, as far as they go, sensible:-

> 1.2 There should be a clearly accepted division of responsibilities at the head of a company, which will ensure a balance of power and authority, such that no one individual has unfettered powers of decision. Where the chairman is also the chief executive, it is essential that there should be a strong and independent element on the board, with a recognised senior member.

> 1.3 The board should include non-executive directors of sufficient calibre and number for their views to carry significant weight in the board's decisions.

As a general rule it is clearly right that the chairman's role should be separate from that of the chief executive. Cadbury says:-

if the two roles are combined in one person, it represents a considerable concentration of power.

We would agree, and there is no shortage of examples in recent times where such a 'concentration of power' can be, and has been, dangerous. Cadbury is certainly right to say that the 'clearly accepted division of responsibilities' should 'ensure a balance of power and authority such that no one individual has unfettered powers of decision'. This, of course, is where non-executive directors come in - or should do, with concomitant powers to express views, and indeed an obligation to do so. Subservient silence is not the solution.

Cadbury CBP (1.4) says:-

The board should have a formal schedule of matters specifically reserved to it for decision to ensure that the direction and control of the company is firmly in their hands.

This follows on from 4.23 and 4.24 of Final Cadbury which contains a valid and useful recommendation that boards should have such a schedule (which well run boards have anyway), and suggests what should at least be included in it, namely:-

(a) acquisition and disposal of assets of the company or its subsidiaries that are material to the company;

(b) investments, capital projects, authority levels, treasury policies, and risk management policies.

This is, surely, a very short list (indeed shorter than that set out in Draft Cadbury) and we believe it should be expanded to include, for a start:-

● bank borrowing facilities, loans, repayment of loans and foreign currency transactions above a certain size (as per Draft Cadbury);

● agreements the terms whereof might inhibit the future freedom of action of the company

● off-balance sheet 'borrowings'

● senior appointments with board prospects

● appointment of the internal auditor

● appointment of merchant banks, brokers, PR agents or any change.

Non-executive directors (NEDs)

Cadbury stops short of laying down a minimal number of NEDs; we propose a mandatory minimal number of one third of the total number of directors. We agree with Cadbury CBP (2.1) which says that NEDs should bring 'an independent judgement to bear on issues of strategy, performance, resources, including key appointments, and standards of conduct'. We also agree that 'the majority should be independent and free from any business or other relationship which could materially interfere with the exercise of their independent judgement, apart from their fees and shareholding'.

As regards the length of tenure of office, Cadbury merely states that NEDs should be appointed for 'specified terms', and that reappointment should not be 'automatic' - but they do not elaborate on what that actually might mean. Our own views on NEDs are set out in some detail in our Code of Practice (see chapter 13 and appendix A), and in appendix B as to their terms.

Cadbury (CBP 1.5) usefully states that 'there should be an agreed procedure for directors to take independent professional advice, if necessary, at the company's expense'. This is to be welcomed, but nowhere does Cadbury show that this has been thought through in detail. There must, of course, be some constraints and coordination (possibly through the NED chairman or deputy chairman), for without such constraints the taking of third party advice could slip into uncontrolled extravagance. Nevertheless, this is a highly sensitive area and there are problems of confidentiality which Cadbury, in both Report and CBP, ignores.

We would illustrate these problems by the following example, (which is purely hypothetical).

Let us suppose that I am a director of X plc and I take the view that something is going wrong on which I wish to obtain a confidential second opinion. I go off, therefore, to see another solicitor, barrister, or a firm of chartered accountants or actuaries - none being the usual advisers to the company. I may not want the company to know, when it reimburses me for the costs, whom I went to see, or what sort of adviser he was, or what I went to see him about. The company, when such reimbursement was requested, would presumably have to see that the expenditure was properly vouched for. Would it be sufficient, for internal or external audit purposes, for me to say that I had taken independent advice on a matter concerning the company, that the costs were £x, and I would be grateful for a cheque at the company's earliest convenience? There is also the spectre of VAT. Moreover, if my independent adviser tells me that there is, in fact, nothing at all to worry about I should still expect to be reimbursed provided that it was appropriate for me to seek independent advice - but would I want the company to know that I had even sought advice in the first place?

This, although a hypothetical example, illustrates a quite serious dilemma, which can only be tackled on a case by case basis between the director concerned and the chairman or deputy chairman who are, hopefully, not involved in the problem and will preserve confidentiality.

Executive directors

CBP (3.1) states that 'directors' service contracts should not exceed three years without shareholder approval'. We would go further and say that service agreements with executive directors must not exceed a fixed term of three years without prior shareholder approval: that rolling notice service agreements, providing for more than twelve months notice of termination by the company, must not be entered into without shareholder approval.

Our recommendations may need legislation to implement; the CBP, likewise, will (as Cadbury accepted) require legislation if the restrictions of length of service agreements with executive directors are to have general applicability - i.e. not just applying to directors of Stock Exchange listed companies.

We would also go further than CBP (3.2) which deals with disclosure of directors' total emoluments and recommend that they, and those of the chairman and the highest paid UK director, should be fully disclosed, differentiating between their salary and any performance related elements. We consider that the directors' report (or, if preferred, a note to the accounts) should fully disclose the emoluments of each and every director (both executive and non-executive) split into their salary and (for executive directors) performance related elements - with the basis upon which performance is measured being explained.

We really cannot see why all emoluments of every director should not be set out in the report and accounts of every London Stock Exchange listed company. After all, we know precisely what top civil servants and judges are paid - the details are in the press. Why should shareholders not know what each of their directors is paid?

CBP (3.3) mentions the work of the remuneration committee, such a committee being made up 'wholly or mainly' of non-executive directors - we say 'wholly'. We discussed the subject of remuneration committees in greater detail in chapter 5.

Controls and reporting

It is perhaps not surprising that the Cadbury Committee, whose mandate put particular emphasis on 'Financial Aspects of Corporate Governance', has performed best in the section of the CBP which deals with controls and reporting (CBP 4.1-4.7). Most of what they say about this topic is well thought out and constructive (see our appendix A, where we have gratefully adopted some of their proposals).

In the body of the Final Cadbury Report (4.35(b)) Cadbury recommend that members of the audit committee should be composed of non-executive directors only. We agree.

We share Cadbury's anxiety in the matter of 'going concern' (Report 5.18-5.22; CBP4.6). We agree that directors (rather than the auditors) should continue to be required to state in their report that the business is a going concern. Already, by implication, auditors are required to confirm in their audit report that (as at the date of that report) the business was a going concern on the accounts date. If that were not the case, the auditors would be required to report specifically if the absence of such a going concern basis would affect the value of the assets or the liabilities of the company.

We are not convinced that an extension of the auditor's responsibilities, so as to require the audit firm to express its own opinion that the business is a going concern, is right or appropriate.

Let us look at Final Cadbury in full in this context (paragraph 5.22) where it said:-

> The Committee recommends that:-
> (a) directors should state in the report and accounts that the business is a going concern, with supporting assumptions or qualifications as necessary;
> (b) the auditors should report on this statement;
> (c) the accountancy profession in conjunction with representatives of preparers of accounts should take the lead in developing guidance for companies and auditors;
> (d) the question of legislation should be decided in the light of experience.

The recommendation, in substance, repeated what was in Draft Cadbury.

Our view is that if auditors (acting independently) decline to report (favourably), on the directors' statement that the business is a going concern, then the company will assuredly not live long, even if it otherwise might have done.

As an alternative, we suggest that consideration might be given to a requirement that the directors' report should state, specifically, whether, in their view, the company's working capital was adequate as at the date the accounts were signed off, with supporting assumptions or qualifications as necessary. The auditors could be required to report on that statement, a task they are often called upon to perform in takeover situations. This issue on the going concern basis, coupled with the paper from the Working Group, was considered earlier in chapter 6.

Before examining the public reactions to the Cadbury Draft Report we would make one further point: English law knows of no distinction (as to duties, responsibilities, knowledge or deemed knowledge) as between executive directors on the one hand and NEDs on the other (except, perhaps, by implication, under the Disqualification Act and, to some extent, under the Insolvency Act). This troubles us and is, we believe, a failure of the law to recognise what happens in fact and what will increasingly happen in fact if a requirement for having a mandatory number of NEDs on the board is to be implemented.

Public reaction to the Draft Cadbury Report

Public reaction to Draft Cadbury was vociferous and came from many quarters: the press, institutional shareholders and fund managers, the accountancy profession, the Institute of Directors, the Confederation of British Industry, and the Stock Exchange itself. Final Cadbury introduced few changes only to the Draft, and a review of reactions to the Draft therefore remains interesting.

General press comment revealed widespread agreement that Government (i.e. legislation) should not become involved, with the caveat that listed companies might well bring new legislation upon themselves if they did not voluntarily improve their practices. Shareholder democracy alone would not suffice to bring this about, and if Cadbury were to have any real success there would have to be enforcement mechanisms.

The press also said that if the Stock Exchange, as a leading City regulator, was unwilling to stiffen its resolve it would have to recognise that the days of self-regulation in the City might well be numbered. We examine the Stock Exchange's reaction later in this chapter and its circulars in chapter 13.

The reaction of industry, as exemplified in what has been said in response to Draft Cadbury by and on behalf of the IOD and CBI, was depressing. If what they have said accurately foretells what industrial companies, enjoying the privilege of a listing on the Stock Exchange, will do - or, rather, not do - in response to Cadbury, then sooner or later there will have to be legislative intervention.

The IOD, having expressed broad sympathy with most of the Draft Cadbury recommendations, said also that they were 'bureaucratic nonsense' which sounded out 'the wrong signal that there should be two groups on a board of directors - the doers and the checkers.' They said Cadbury was sending a false message that there was 'something wrong' in Britain's boardrooms, and were critical of Cadbury's suggestions that shareholders and auditors should become involved in corporate governance issues. The following particularly significant quotation can, we think, be left to speak for itself:-

> The responsibility for running companies is that of the boards of directors; shareholders and auditors do have their role in relation to the running of a company but questions of corporate governance are determined in the boardroom.
>
> *Peter Morgan, Director-General IOD*
> *Letter to The Financial Times published 31 July 1992*

Another specific criticism the IOD had of Cadbury is that the 'policing' role of NEDs, and Cadbury's desire to impose special functions on them, would undermine the principle of the unitary board and emphasise too much the need to 'supervise' boards, rather than being positive about their role. They did not want to see a drift towards a two-tier board split between management and supervision: nor do we - see chapter 4. And they were worried about the Code becoming a listing requirement: we are convinced it must, but with a stronger, clearer, and more mandatory basis (see chapter 13 and appendix A).

The CBI, who were represented on the Cadbury Committee, publicly welcomed the Draft Report as an important contribution to the debate on corporate governance. This did not, however, prevent them from expressing a barrage of dissent which makes interesting reading.

They have:-

- opposed proposals to make the Committee's recommendations enforceable;
- objected to the proposed Stock Exchange listing agreement since it would lead to more bureaucracy;
- been critical of the monitoring proposals and special duties assigned to NEDs;
- whilst supporting in principle the Code of Best Practice, rejected plans for its enforcement;

- said that shareholders were best placed to enforce a voluntary code on corporate governance and need no help from auditors, the Stock Exchange or NEDs;
- objected to the suggestion that NEDs should police the executives, and said that all directors should work as a team with equal legal duties and obligations;
- objected to there being a listing requirement that companies should disclose the extent to which they comply with the Cadbury CBP;
- said that the CBP gives too much power to the NEDs;
- said that the membership of the audit committee should not be limited to NEDs;
- said that they can give little support to the suggestion that the NEDs should appoint a leader;
- questioned the Committee's views that there is an ample supply of qualified part time directors to serve as NEDs;
- expressed strong reservations about the compliance statement being a condition of listing.

Whilst being represented on the Committee, and ostensibly welcoming the Committee's Draft Report, the CBI nevertheless contradicted every substantial recommendation that it made.

Institutional shareholders and fund managers quite understandably felt that Cadbury's form of voluntarism was inadequate and unlikely to work. They also felt that the Report fell short of what was needed to improve corporate governance. We agree.

Moving on to the accountancy profession, we find the Institute of Chartered Accountants in England and Wales expressing 'serious misgivings' about auditors certifying that companies had followed the Code simply because this is not a task which, even with the best will in the world, they can fulfil. The Auditing Practices Board has said that the certification requirement is 'impracticable', and recommends that the audit committee might be a better body to certify compliance.

CIMA (the Chartered Institute of Management Accountants) judged the Cadbury proposals to be laudable but weak. They felt that the issue of internal controls had not been properly addressed, and, understandably enough, urged a strengthening of the internal audit system. They recommended that the CBP be made mandatory, that interim financial statements should be audited and believed that, unless the CBP were to be made compulsory, companies which are not well run would simply ignore it. With all that the accountancy profession says we most heartily agree.

Another independent submission to Cadbury apparently expressed the view that, without more robust enforcement than Cadbury envisages, the few companies disinclined to adopt good standards of corporate governance would simply go on as before.

Finally it is instructive to examine the reaction of the Stock Exchange. This, to say the least, is disappointing, somewhat tangled, and decidedly ambivalent. Not only was the Stock Exchange a sponsor of the Cadbury Committee, but its chairman, Sir Andrew Hugh-Smith, was a member of the Committee. He has said:-

We believe that this Report, by codifying best practice and ensuring that companies have to account publicly for their compliances, will prove a helpful means of maintaining and raising standards.

On the face of it, this constitutes an unqualified endorsement, and Sir Andrew went on to say that the implementation of Cadbury depended on 'the wholehearted commitment of all involved in any way with corporate governance.' But he has also said that the Stock Exchange 'will continue to regard the board, collectively and individually, as wholly responsible for the conduct of a listed or quoted company's affairs'. There should be no sanctions for non-compliers but the Stock Exchange may 'blacklist' persistent offenders.

It must be true to say that the body most likely to be involved in corporate governance is the Stock Exchange, but their expressed 'wholehearted commitment' to Cadbury should not be taken too readily at its face value. On the **positive** side the Stock Exchange has said that as a condition of listing they would consider adopting the inclusion of balance sheet information with interim statements. They have also endorsed the proposal for a listing requirement under which companies will have to disclose the extent to which they comply with the CBP, and have gone further in saying that companies which do not comply will have to explain themselves.

On the other hand they have said that the Stock Exchange would be unlikely to do more than censure companies for failure to comply.

Significantly, the Stock Exchange has tried to postpone a serious consideration of corporate governance issues. They have said they would welcome a review of the Code's effectiveness **after two years**, and hope to be part of the review process. In the meantime they say they will meet representatives of leading institutional shareholders 'to discover what features of the Code are of particular interest to them and where non-compliance by companies in which they hold stakes would prompt them to take action.'

Eventually an element of realism was shown when the Stock Exchange said:-

> If companies do not comply [with the Code] voluntarily, then political
> pressure will be brought to bear to force more disclosure.

We are certain that the Stock Exchange would not wish to have legislation to 'force more disclosure' but their current position on the fence will have that obvious outcome. Legislation is not, in our view, the right answer but in the light of the attitudes initially displayed by the CBI, by the IOD and by the Stock Exchange, it may sadly be inevitable.

The view taken by the Stock Exchange seems to be that responsibility for taking action to improve corporate governance remains with the shareholders but they generally lack the 'clout' or the will to enforce their suggestions on boards who might disagree with them. We strongly hold the view that no self-regulatory system will work unless there is from the top downwards both an acknowledgement that the Code addresses the right issues in the right way, and a determination to encourage the implementation of its provisions, supported by a Code in clear and enforceable language, a Code which is incorporated in the Yellow Book. To make such enforcements work, there will have to be sanctions upon defaulting directors available to the Stock Exchange and seen to be imposed by it.

Otherwise, there will have to be legislation and, protest as they might, the CBI and the IOD will have brought it upon themselves, their members and us all.

The Final Cadbury Report

The final version of the Cadbury Report was published on 1 December 1992. It was subjected, predictably, to very close scrutiny by financial journalists and institutional and private investors.

Following the appearance of the Draft Report at the end of May 1992 a period of two months was allowed for the submission of comments from individuals or corporate bodies, and in Appendix 7 of the Final Report there appears an impressively long list of those who took advantage of this, among them the authors of this book.

It has to be said, with regret, that the Cadbury Report and (above all) its Code of Best Practice outstandingly illustrate the principle of missed opportunities. In 1.7 (Draft 1.6) the report persists in saying 'The basic system of corporate governance ("financial corporate governance" in the Draft) is sound'. But in 7.3 it says '... *it is widely accepted that standards in the corporate sector have to be raised*'. Surely, this can only mean that while most companies are well aware of proper, open and seemly methods of corporate governance, too many of them are falling short of putting these methods adequately into practice, and being covert about the inadequacies.

Cadbury clearly accepts this, but fails to be sufficiently tough about it. A reasonable analogy might be drawn with the rugby football referees who, confronted with persistent, serious and flagrant breaches of the laws of the game, hold back from the ultimate (and perfectly correct) sanction of sending the offenders off the field and resort instead to a finger-wagging reprimand. Sadly there is a great deal of finger-wagging in Cadbury.

The report shows a touching belief in the perfectability of inadequate boards by even suggesting that a **voluntary** system of self-regulation is going to be sufficient to cleanse Augean stables. The tendency to spread responsibility for corporate governance (3.14) too thinly over the institutions and the media as well as boards, gives an unsatisfactory and inadequate lead and stimulus for improvement, when what is clearly needed is a strong and unambiguous Code of Practice (with sanctions that hurt the offending directors rather than their shareholders) which will more readily and manifestly be complied with by boards of companies.

Institutions have a consistent record of a reluctance to interfere. Fund managers thrive (or otherwise) on their financial track record, rather than on their prowess in enforcing or encouraging good corporate governance on the companies in which they invest. It is naive to think this will ever change, although there has been isolated (and little publicised) examples which are encouraging.

Shrewd and keenly investigative financial journalists who might have doubts about a particular company's conduct still have a useful 'whistle-blowing' function, but they have no actual responsibility for **forcing compliance with the Code**. Ultimately, only the board can have that, and it must be an obligation, rather than a lame imprecise exhortation.

A closer look at specific sections of the Final Report reveals a number of changes in emphasis from the Draft:-

Paragraph 1.8 seems to be responding to pressure from the CBI and the IOD in stressing the need for unitary and not 'two-tier' boards, and this is developed further in 4.1 to 4.6. We see no logic behind the fears which have been expressed that the requirement for a strong element of NEDs would lead to a quasi 'two-tier' board. The (unitary) board, under the cohesive and constructive leadership of the chairman can, and in our experience does, work as a unitary team despite - perhaps even because of - there being a number of experienced and respected NEDs on the board. Good executive directors welcome astute and probing questions from the NEDs; they do not resent them. We have never personally encountered a 'them and us' atmosphere, or a feeling that we, as NEDs, have been resentfully regarded as the 'checkers' of the 'doers'.

Paragraph 4.9 repeats the Draft Report's perfectly correct statement of the principle that chairmen and chief executives should be separate people, but with an odd weakening of the specific recommendation. The **Draft** at this point said that where the two roles were combined 'it is essential that there should be a strong, independent element on the board, *with an appointed leader*' and this was repeated in the Draft CBP. In the report itself the 'appointed leader' has disappeared, to surface far more vaguely in the CBP as 'a recognised senior member'. This is surely too ill defined to be of much real value, but we do not see much need for 'an appointed leader' either.

4.17 is a new paragraph on whether the supply of NEDs is sufficient to meet demand. The best that Cadbury can do is to promulgate the limited suggestion that executive directors of some companies could become NEDs of others 'to increase the pool of potential NEDs'. This is self-evident but would not reassure the critical shareholder because it sounds suspiciously like the 'old boy network' at its fell work. Furthermore it entirely ignores what Andrew Jack, writing in The Financial Times (4 December 1992) points out: that PRO NED has a list of some 1,600 potential candidates, that few companies are recruiting NEDs from external sources, and that 'only about 30% of companies use a formal search process to identify candidates'. Cadbury has missed an excellent opportunity to address this problem with any crisp advice or recommendations.

Paragraph 4.35(g) represents, as a number of commentators were not slow to spot, a significant weakening of the last point in Draft 4.29. The chairman of the audit committee now merely has 'to be **available**' to answer questions at the annual general meeting rather than be 'responsible' for answering.

The same near emasculation has been suffered by the chairman of the remuneration committee in 4.44. 4.44 on board remuneration is still inadequate in respect of disclosure. This matter was tackled in some depth by Christopher Lorenz in The Financial Times (4 December 1992). He looks at the 'yawning gulf' between, on the one hand, Cadbury's 'puny' **recommendations** in the CBP and, on the other, the 'fully-blown **regulations**' of the US Securities and Exchange Commission which run to three pages with charts and notes. Nevertheless, in fairness to Cadbury, and to show the extent of the task facing reformers in this area, it must be said (as Lorenz points out) that only **eight** of the FTSE 100 companies currently complied with Cadbury guidelines.

On **pensions governance** (4.60 Final; 4.51 Draft) the report temporises, using the advent of the Report of Professor Goode's Pension Law Review Committee as a convenient excuse for failing to state even a few basic principles. This is another opportunity missed, and we would again refer to our own suggested Code of Practice (see chapter 13 and appendix A).

A number of recommendations have been put onto the back burner for two years (1995) when Cadbury's proposed successor body 'may wish to review or consider [them] in greater depth', namely:-

- Code of Best Practice as it applies to smaller companies;
- Directors' training;
- Rules for disclosure of directors' remuneration, and shareholders' role in this;
- Inclusion of cash flow information in interim reports;
- Procedures for putting forward resolutions at general meetings;
- Nature and extent of auditors' liability.

In respect of NEDs' entitlement or otherwise to share options and pension scheme, the **Report** (4.13) says it is 'good practice' for NEDs to have no participation - and we agree. But the **Code** itself is totally silent on this, which we find indefensible. This topic, and others of similar importance, are mysteriously relegated to 'Notes' on p.9 of the CBP, which seems to suggest that while the Cadbury Committee considers them to be all 'good practice', they do not even have the status of 'best' practice. But why not?

Among comments in the press, some of the most pungent came from The Investors' Chronicle (4 December 1992) which in a customarily brief editorial stated that self-regulation was, in fact, a contradiction in terms, going on to say that while Cadbury was 'full of perfectly reasonable ideas' it offered 'no sanctions against those whose stewardship for their investors falls short'. The editor felt, as do we ourselves, that without sanctions aimed at the people who are really accountable, it will once again and as usual be the 'ordinary investors and customers' who will suffer.

We can only feel that Cadbury was a worthy and well intentioned exercise, but has proved to have been largely unsuccessful, inadequate and toothless in attaining its objectives. Theoretically it is still possible for the fraudulent, unscrupulous, or simply incompetent to comply by merely paying lip service to a flabby vague Code. This is really not good enough. The Committee's successors, in 1995, will have a great deal more to do, if not by then pre-empted by reason of the manifest inadequacies of its predecessors.

This being said, it is encouraging to see an increasing number of listed companies following Cadbury. We continue to commend a less optional and vague exhortation. We hope many will follow our more exacting and more demanding Code of Practice. Those who do not should not attract the same level of acclaim and support, and their directors should ask themselves 'Why?' and personally take the consequences.

13 The way ahead

Our suggested 'Code of Practice'

Sir Adrian Cadbury, in the preface to the December 1992 Cadbury report, summarises the reasons why the press, the City and shareholders are focusing on corporate governance:-

> The harsh economic climate is partly responsible, since it has exposed company reports and accounts to unusually close scrutiny. It is, however, the continuing concern about standards of financial reporting and accountability, heightened by BCCI, Maxwell and the controversy over directors' pay, which has kept corporate governance in the public eye.

> Unexpected though this attention may have been, it reflects a climate of opinion which accepts that changes are needed, and it presents an opportunity to raise standards of which we should take full advantage.

What are the expectations of the City, shareholders and the press about corporate governance? They surely go further than a desire to avoid spectacular failures, or to stop the concentration of too much power in the hands of one man. Corporate governance does not only feature in the press when excessive pay awards to directors are made, or when shareholders suffer financially as a result of a company failure. A consensus is developing as to positive standards of corporate governance which should form part of a structure for success, going further than inhibiting disasters, greed and clear wrongdoing.

The need for increased numbers of NEDs and the importance of the roles they are to play are being recognised by shareholders, by the press and even within the boardroom. Calls for more openness and for greater accountability are frequent and irresistible. Yet industry remains generally reluctant to respond, fearing the birth of a quasi two-tier board with what they call the doers and the checkers. The root causes for this reluctance are probably a fear of some loss of executive control and an apprehension that too much formalisation and consultation may hamper the company's ability to act. Neither the objective of increasing shareholder value nor the capacity of the company to act dynamically should be held up or inhibited by the adoption of effective corporate governance practices. Indeed, the positive contribution such practices can bring to the adoption of sound and thought out policies and strategies and their implementation and monitoring should enhance, not detract from, a company's ability to perform competitively. Building a corporate culture where there is mutual understanding of, and respect for, the different tasks and emphases of executive and non-executive directors respectively becomes a crucial part of the exercise.

Previous solutions have not worked. Even with the recent Stock Exchange requirement to state which provisions of Cadbury have been met, the CBP remains too vague, too subjective and too optional for adequate standards of corporate governance to be achieved generally. Although the vast majority of UK companies are run well and with integrity, all is still not well in the field of corporate governance. Cadbury stressed that the bulk of its recommendations should be taken as representing current best practice. In our view, it is neither current, nor best: merely a modest start.

For corporate governance to move forward, two vital steps must be taken. One is to compile an appropriate Code of Practice - one which clarifies positive standards of practice across a much broader and well defined spectrum than Cadbury's Code of Best Practice. The board's role should be involved in overseeing all activities of the company - financial, personnel, legal and environmental amongst them - and must be clearly and acceptably defined. Secondly, adherence to the provisions of such a Code must also be made obligatory at least for all listed companies, those to seek a listing, and others with 'outside' shareholders, so that a common standard of corporate governance becomes not only generally acknowledged but also practised.

In this book, we have discussed the current legal background, current practice, Cadbury's recommendations and the listing obligations of the Stock Exchange, highlighting where they all fall short. Our Suggested Code of Practice (SCP) in appendix A gives a detailed alternative to Cadbury's Code of Best Practice, closing some of the gaps which Cadbury's provisions left. Some of Cadbury is, however, reflected in our SCP.

The SCP deals with the following topics:-
- the constitution of the board;
- board committees;
- the functioning of a board; and
- the board and its accountability.

A brief summary of its recommendations here gives its flavour and the reasons behind our suggestions.

The constitution of the board

The SCP deals first with the minimum number of NEDs on the board, and recommends that at least a third of the total number of directors shall be non-executive. NEDs should also be free of any other business or financial connection with the company except as shareholders. The chairman should preferably be an NED; he should preferably not also be chief executive or managing director. When appointing a new NED, boards should look for objectivity and a breadth of experience which enhances the present composition of the board. The SCP stresses the crucial roles of the NEDs in monitoring compliance with its provisions, and also as a group acting as monitors of the performance and ability of executive directors.

NEDs should be appointed initially for three years. The terms of their appointment should be laid out in a letter (we provide a suggested proforma in appendix B). The terms should cover the NED's duties, time involvement, fees and the procedure for reimbursing expenses including seeking independent advice as appropriate. The level of fees for NEDs should reflect their predicted time commitment and responsibility; their remuneration should not be fixed so generously as to jeopardise their independence.

The process of selection of NEDs should be a formal one, led by the NED chairman or deputy chairman, conducted through the appropriate committee. All appointments should be approved by the board. Prior to appointment, NED candidates should be provided with relevant information. A checklist is set out in appendix D.

Service agreements with executive directors should not exceed three years without prior shareholder approval. These should be renegotiable in the third year, so that continuity can be provided if appropriate. Rolling notice service agreements which provide for more than twelve months notice of termination by the company should again only be entered into with prior approval from shareholders. Each director must maintain a directors' and officers' (D&O) insurance policy to cover his position with the company; the premium should be reimbursed by the company.

Board committees

This section states that all boards should set up both an audit and a remuneration committee, both composed entirely of NEDs. It then deals with the duties and responsibilities of these committees, and their relationship with the board.

Reporting from committees to the board should be through the company secretary; directors not on the relevant committee can only attend its meetings by invitation from that committee. The audit committee's responsibilities are also clearly defined in SCP - including reviewing the choice of the accountancy firm working with the company on consultancy matters. The remuneration committee's responsibilities are also clearly defined; they include the regular commissioning of an independent report from external management consultants on executive appraisals and remuneration packages, and the level of NED fees.

Other committees may be appropriate from time to time, company by company, either on an ad hoc (e.g. project related) basis, or as standing committees. Since these will be set up to fulfil a special corporate purpose, we do not cover them in SCP.

The functioning of the board

The primary initiative for this is the chairman's and the company secretary's. This is, again, amplified in detail in appendix A.

The organisation of corporate groups is of relevance here. We include a recommendation that each major trading division or subsidiary should make a presentation to the board annually, involving the attendance of divisional and subsidiary managers at board meetings.

The board should devise and adopt a regime for the division of executive responsibilities; no individual should have unfettered powers of decision - levels of responsibility should always be clearly defined by the board.

There should be adopted a schedule of matters to be reserved for Board approval, and we set out in appendix E an Aide Memoire for adaptation to accord with and reflect the company's activities, size and plans.

The board's accountability

This section proposes that each director should have a legal obligation as a primary duty to ensure that attention is publicly drawn to any matter which falls short of proper expectations. By including such a proposal, we are suggesting that, in the absence of an appropriate corporate announcement or statements, each director should regard it as his personal duty, if necessary, to make public any reservations he has, even if disclosure might prove detrimental to the company's market position and to shareholders. No director will (or should) rush into making a personal statement. He will need to be convinced not only that the issue is one of substantial importance (e.g. to counter any risk of a false market being created or subsisting), but also that he has used every effort to persuade the board itself to do what is appropriate and has told the chairman what he feels and that he has no alternative but to say so, and has taken appropriate advice. We propose the adoption of this obligation as a legal requirement (legislation may be necessary) to counter the argument that, because of each director's duty to act in the best interests of the company, making any personal statement at all may constitute a breach of that duty.

The second recommendation is also a vital part of shifting and defining responsibilities for corporate governance. Section 4.2 of our SCP makes a compliance statement obligatory - to be included with the directors' report and the annual accounts. This statement must give details as to the extent of compliance with the **mandatory** requirements of the Code. If all the requirements have not been met, details should be given, and reasons for non-compliance. Supporting legislation, again, may be necessary for we would suggest there be a requirement for a shareholders' meeting to consider the situation (compare s142 CA85 where there is a serious loss of capital).

Emoluments for each and every director (not merely grouped figures) should be disclosed, split into salary and (for executive directors) performance-related pay. The basis on which performance is measured should be summarised.

Boards of companies with pension funds should include in the directors' report a statement of their policy, and their attitude towards funding. A statement naming the fund's trustees, administrators and holders should be mandatory; the investment manager(s) should also be named. Any connection of any of these people with a director or with a major shareholder (3% plus) should also be disclosed. Some of the pension trustees should be current NEDs. The company should not itself be a trustee. The administrator should not also be the custodian.

Periodical environmental and management audits should be commissioned, and shareholders should be told that this practice is adopted and implemented. The results of such audits must be treated as confidential. Shareholders cannot expect them to be revealed, but often professional advisers (e.g. the auditors particularly as to the environmental audit) might appropriately have access to the reports.

Providing a Code of Practice gives directors a blueprint - it does not ensure that such practices will be universally accepted and kept. Directors who are faced with a conflict as to compliance with the SCP or other fundamental matters which they cannot internally resolve, can still be put in a position where their only choice is to resign - and that poses the ultimate dilemma.

There are, of course, many ways of resolving conflict before resignation - and every step should be taken before resignation. The chairman of the board has a responsibility to ensure that differences are handled well; compromise is often possible with a change of emphasis in a resolution. Any director who feels unable to agree with the majority at a meeting should first consult the chairman, to see if he can suggest a possible solution. Failing that, he should seek outside professional advice - at the company's expense. After taking such advice, he should then discuss the conflict again with the chairman and, if necessary, the board. A circular letter after full discussion (probably with the chairman) explaining the dissenting director's position is an option, although one which he might have to finance himself. An individual director also has some ability, on a confidential basis, to bring pressure to bear from outside. He can appeal to major institutional shareholders for support in his conflict; there may even be grounds for him to inform the Stock Exchange if he feels that their sanction is appropriate. Resignation should be a last resort, taken only when every other avenue has been explored. Making the conflict public is, perhaps, the penultimate resort.

Examples of such dilemmas are not difficult to find. A new NED, invited to join the board because of his reputation in another field, might well find that aspects of the company's management plans (e.g. proposed board changes) or of its current financial reporting and accounting are inadequate, or worse, are inconsistent with what he was told prior to appointment. A decision to resign, even without publicly stating reasons, shortly after appointment, would signal to the Stock Market and to the public that something was awry. If our recommendations over a checklist for new directors are followed, NEDs joining a board should be less vulnerable to such a dilemma.

Even when faced with less contentious issues than finance, a director can also find there are problems in acting in what he genuinely and properly believes are the best interests of the company. Take, as an example, a chief executive who is also chairman of the board, and is ageing fast. His personal wishes are to hold on to the company; he expresses a deep reluctance to find a successor. The company desperately needs new blood - decisions are being taken inappropriately, or too slowly, for the company to thrive or even survive. A director on that company's board will find it easier to handle any conflict he has with the personal loyalties of long-standing directors if he has the support of major shareholders in trying to prompt the chief executive's retirement. Our recommendation that the chairman and the chief executive should not be the same person removes this conflict from the personal sphere - the chairman of the board can introduce succession planning earlier in the day, before such a problem arises.

If important decisions on corporate governance rely on the personal integrity of each and every director, and conflict cannot be resolved within the board meeting, or by direct consultation with the Chairman, a director has little choice but to resign. Yet for any director, this poses a genuine conflict - resignation is often portrayed as acting contrary to his duties as a director. As a director, he has a duty to act in the best interests of the company's shareholders. If, in the process of explaining the reasons for his resignation, a director exposes information which decreases the market value of shares, it can be said he is not facing his responsibilities to the company's owners - the shareholders - and is not carrying through the tasks for which he was appointed. Yet to stay could be a compromise of his own integrity, if behaviour contrary to accepted legal, financial or corporate standards was occurring.

This dilemma - the harm to the company's position versus the truth - is one which directors do face given the present ill-defined and inadequately monitored and enforced standards of corporate governance. Cadbury's decision to make their Code of Best Practice voluntary, and their reluctance to break much new ground, combine to place heavy but vague responsibilities particularly on the shoulders of NEDs. So does the Stock Exchange's Yellow Book in its continuing obligations (see, further, below). A director who keeps quiet about shortcomings in corporate governance, and toes the party line is less liable to be criticised in the short term than one who brings them to the public eye. Unless the individual director can show that he acted to remedy the situation as soon as he was aware of it, he will be publicly answerable for any misdemeanour, and perhaps legally too, in the longer term.

Monitoring, not legislation

Cadbury has recommended voluntary adherence to its Code of Best Practice; the Stock Exchange has bolstered this by expanding continuing obligations with reference to the CBP.

The London Stock Exchange issued two circulars to company secretaries of listed and USM companies on 23 April 1993 and 8 July 1993.

The earlier of these two circulars added to the continuing obligations of listed companies incorporated in the United Kingdom a requirement to state in its annual report and accounts for accounting periods ending after 30 June 1993, whether or not it had complied throughout the accounting period with Cadbury's Code of Best Practice. It went on to say that a company that had only complied during part of an accounting period, must specify the paragraphs in the CBP with which it had not complied and to give reasons for any non-compliance. Further, the circular required that the company's statement of compliance **must** be reviewed by the auditors before publication insofar as it relates to certain specified paragraphs of the CBP.

Many of these specified paragraphs seem to require auditors to place themselves almost, as it were, in the boardroom alongside the directors if the auditors are, in any meaningful way, to review the company's compliance therewith. Of the specified CBP paragraphs upon which a review by auditors is called for, are:-

- that the board should have a formal schedule of matters specifically reserved to it for decision to ensure that the direction and control of the company is firmly in its hands (1.4);
- that there should be an agreed procedure for directors to take independent professional advice, if necessary at the company's expense (1.5);
- that non-executive directors are appointed for specified terms and reappointment should not be automatic (2.3);
- that non-executive directors should be selected through a formal process, this process and their appointment being matters for the board as a whole (2.4);
- that directors' service contracts should not exceed three years without shareholder approval (3.1); and
- that executive directors' pay should be subject to the recommendations of a remuneration committee made up wholly or mainly of non-executive directors (3.3). We take the view that the matters listed above are wholly improperly regarded as part of the auditor's remit.

The other specified paragraphs can perhaps more readily be accepted as falling within the fields of influence (if not responsibility) of the auditors, namely:-

- that there should be a full and clear disclosure of directors' **total** emoluments and those of the chairman and the highest paid UK director, including pension contributions and stock options, and with separate figures for salary and performance related elements and with the basis on which performance is measured being explained (3.2);
- that the board has established an audit committee of at least three non-executive directors with clear written terms of reference (4.3);
- that the directors should explain their responsibility for preparing the accounts next to a statement by the auditors about their reporting responsibilities (4.4);
- that the directors should report on the effectiveness of the company's system of internal control (4.5); and
- that directors should report that the business is a going concern, with supporting assumptions or qualifications as necessary (4.6).

We have commented above (adversely) on the proposed involvement of the auditors directly in the going concern report.

The points raised under CBP 4.5 and 4.6 are stated, in Note 13 to the CBP, as those with which companies 'will not be able to comply' until guidance has been developed by the accountancy profession: a fine excuse for delay, but flabby again.

The second circular, dated 8 July 1993, modifies the application of the requirements in the first circular to a company's first financial period ending after 30 June 1993. Companies reporting on their first financial year ending after 30 June 1993 may limit their statement of compliance to that part of the financial year which begins after that date.

Finally, the first such circular says this:-

> The Exchange does not see it as part of its own role to pass judgement on whether the extent of a company's compliance with the Code is adequate or not, but it may make public any company's failure to make the required statement.

The present statement by the Stock Exchange, quoted above, is understandable enough in the context of a voluntary code which is loosely and imprecisely worded and where the whole question of compliance or non-compliance is put on a voluntary basis. But we do not consider that such a basis is in any way adequate. If a Code of Practice such as we set out in appendix A were to be introduced as part of a company's continuing obligations, we would urge the Stock Exchange to take a somewhat more robust approach in passing judgement on non-compliance. If the Stock Exchange does not monitor compliance with the Code, who will do so?

The second circular ends with an exhortation that 'both the Cadbury Committee and the Exchange would like to encourage companies to give a statement of compliance for the financial year as a whole'.

This is still not sufficient. Voluntary self-regulation is not going to prove to be enough. To ensure that good corporate governance occurs, some system of monitoring (with appropriate sanctions) will be necessary; failing that, legislation.

Legislation would have grave disadvantages - the requirements in many spheres (financial, legal, environmental) are changing fast. Any law could only encapsulate requirements which quickly become outdated.

The functioning of the Takeover Panel provides a useful example of flexible but efficient non-statutory regulation. Its powers and responsibilities are sufficiently well defined to ensure adherence to the spirit of the Takeover Code;

the system has strength combined with flexibility. It can be readily and swiftly changed to adapt to changes in the market place. But it is objective. The Cadbury CBP is subjective for each company to comply with as it sees fit.

So we suggest a different, and firmer approach outlined in our criticisms of Cadbury in chapter 12. The Stock Exchange already has 'continuing obligations' for existing listings defined in the Yellow Book in Section 5; it also has power to define qualification requirements for new listings. We propose that eligibility for new listings is linked to an historical adherence to a Code of Practice. Unless the applicant company has substantially adhered to such a Code of Practice for two full accounting periods prior to listing, the application should not be looked upon with favour. A stronger, clearer and more mandatory Code of Practice (perhaps along the lines of appendix A) should also be made part of the continuing obligations, being added to Section 5 of the Yellow Book.

Sanctions

We take the firm and radical view that, after expiry of a transitional period, if the board of an existing listed company continues without reasonable excuse to disregard the mandatory fiats in the Code, then the directors at fault should risk being disqualified (perhaps after a further, limited and discretionary, period of grace) from serving as directors of **any** London Stock Exchange listed company unless they can show cause why they, individually, should not be so disqualified. It may be difficult to prove that some only of the directors are 'at fault', and a procedure might have to be developed for ascertaining the main culprits, otherwise a company might find itself, overnight as it were, without a board. However, we believe and trust that with such potential sanctions available, the level of adherence to the Code will become almost universal. Our 'firm and radical' view is not, perhaps, as novel as it may at first appear.

We now have (since April 1992) Yellow Book (page 1.04) sanctions against directors whose conduct is 'such that in the opinion of the Stock Exchange the retention of office by him is prejudicial to the interests of investors'. In that event it 'will say so publicly; and if the director remains in office the company's securities may be suspended and delisted'.

We would adopt that thinking for breaches of the Code, and go further with a general Stock Exchange (as opposed to legislative) disqualification for directors in the first place. We concede that such a procedure is not without difficulties, but it is undoubtedly better than censure of the (innocent) shareholders through the invocation (albeit reluctantly) by the Stock Exchange, of their sanction of imposing a suspension of dealings in shares of the company in question. Even so, such a sanction - because of the manifest vagueness of Cadbury's proposals and its CBP - looks almost impossible to enforce as things stand.

Consider Final Cadbury (3.10):-

> The Code is to be followed by individuals and companies **in the light of their own particular circumstances**. They are responsible for ensuring that their actions meet the spirit of the Code and in interpreting it they should give precedence to the substance over form. (The bold print is ours.)

It is surely not impossible to lay down that some at least of the provisions of any Code of Practice should be mandatory requirements for **all listed companies**. Others, certainly and inevitably, will have to be standards which are adaptable to the particular type of company involved - but each company should identify them, state what they are, and (publicly) affirm that they have adopted them, or if they have not adopted them, state why.

The advocating of interpretation in accordance with 'the spirit of the Code' again suggests parallels with the Takeover Code, where again precedence is given to substance over form. But with the Takeover Code it is the Panel which interprets this precedence rather than the companies with which the Panel deals. It has to be so if the Takeover Code is to have any effect.

Some minimal but important changes to legislation will be necessary. The period of directors' service agreements needs to be reduced as Cadbury suggested but we would go further, and recommend also that no rolling notice period should exceed twelve months without prior shareholder approval. The distinction, already established in practice but not yet defined in law, between executive directors and NEDs perhaps needs to be acknowledged, although this is not without difficulties both in perception and drafting. A new provision (analogous to s142 of the Companies Act 1985), requiring the convening of an extraordinary general meeting to consider the situation if the mandatory provisions of the Code of Practice are consistently being disregarded, should also perhaps be introduced for all public limited companies, whether or not listed.

Shared responsibility

Any new codified system of corporate governance should be focussed on the constitution and activities of boards of directors. The responsibility for good corporate governance cannot end there. As became evident in our earlier chapters, best practice requires that every component of our matrix faces his own individual responsibility and meets the full obligations of his role.

Responsibilities and obligations also permeate lower down the management structure. If a group is large and diverse, all senior management staff share some responsibility for good corporate governance. Internal audit teams are emphasised in Cadbury - they are a vital component of corporate governance. Reporting lines must be short, robust and responsive. Monitoring and control systems must be effective, not just on the financial side but in the fields of law, environment, pensions and human resources. Ultimately, though, the responsibility must start and stop with the board.

If a director knows that one of his primary obligations is to ensure that the company complies with the mandatory requirements of the Code of Practice, and confirms that he is doing so in the annual accounts by way of a compliance statement, his duties, his fulfilment of them and their priority become more clear cut. An adequate Code of Practice imposes on all directors the individual responsibility for maintaining the integrity of corporate governance; it also sets a standard to which all directors must adhere. Directors who wish to continue to be eligible to serve on the boards of listed public companies will then know the mandatory requirements. The sanction of suspending dealings in a company's shares should surely only be used as a last resort - it hurts the shareholders more than anyone, and their responsibility for corporate governance has been delegated to the board. The ultimate sanctions should be against an individual director. The potential loss of eligibility to be a director of any listed company should be sufficient to encourage compliance by directors.

Corporate governance is a shared responsibility of us all, including shareholders, but the buck stops in the boardroom.

A Suggested code of practice

To be adopted and complied with by the boards:-

(a) of all companies (domestic and foreign) with shares listed on the London Stock Exchange ('Listed Companies') as part of their continuing obligations;

(b) of all companies contemplating a listing in the near future;

(c) of all companies to which the Takeover Code applies; and

(d) of unlisted companies with a significant shareholding in the hands of banks or other financial institutions, or with a wide spread of shareholders.

Note

Mandatory requirements are indicated by use of the word 'shall'. The word 'should' indicates preferred practices.

1.   The constitution of the board

1.1   Each listed company shall have a minimum number of non-executive directors (NEDs) on its board. The minimum shall be one third of the total number of directors, and the majority of the NEDs should be free of any other business or financial connection with the company, apart from their shareholdings. If a listed company falls below that minimum (due to death, disqualification, retirement, removal by the company in general meeting, or resignation) a reasonable time should be given to fill the vacancy or vacancies.

1.2   The chairman should be a NED. He should not also be chief executive or managing director. Where there are felt (by the board after due consideration) to be good reasons for these preferences not to be adopted, one of the NEDs shall be appointed as deputy chairman.

1.3   The NEDs should have the qualities of independence, objectivity and experience to enable them to evaluate the progress of the company and the performance and ability of the executive directors, as well as to contribute in an informed and constructive approach to board discussions. Whilst compliance with this Code shall be a matter for each and every director, the NEDs have a particular role to play in monitoring such compliance. NEDs should, individually, visit all major trading divisions or subsidiaries as soon as practicable after appointment and also periodically thereafter.

1.4   NEDs should typically be appointed for an initial term (subject to ratification by the shareholders) of three years, subsequently renewable by rotation. Each NED should have a letter of appointment setting out his duties, his predicted time involvement, his fees, and the procedure for reimbursement of his expenses on company business, including travel and, where appropriate, for seeking independent professional advice. NEDs shall not be eligible to participate in the company's pension, share option schemes or be included within any class of beneficiaries under a share ownership trust or plan. NEDs' remuneration shall not be performance or project related. Their fees should be at a level not only to reflect their predicted time commitment, but also the level of responsibility undertaken and the number and nature of board committees on which they serve. The level of fees for an NED should not be so high as to jeopardise his independence. NEDs should not be provided with a company car for their personal use. The letters of appointment of NEDs shall be available for inspection by shareholders on request, and at each AGM.

1.5   NEDs should be selected through a formal process. The selection process should be led by the NED chairman or NED deputy chairman and primarily be conducted by the remuneration committee. Information appertaining to the company and its businesses should be provided to candidates in confidence prior to appointment. Appointments must be approved by the board.

1.6   Service agreements with executive directors shall not without prior shareholder approval exceed a fixed term of three years (renegotiable in the third year of the term (but not, formally, before then) so as to provide continuity when required). Rolling notice service agreements, providing for more than twelve months notice of termination by the company, shall not be entered into without prior shareholder approval.

1.7   Each director (including NEDs) shall maintain a directors' and officers' (D&O) insurance policy to cover his own position with the company. The company should effectively reimburse the costs of the premium, grossed up to take account of such costs being subject to tax. The chairman shall be responsible for monitoring compliance by each director with this paragraph.

2.   Board committees

2.1.1 Each listed company shall (by board resolution) set up and shall maintain:-
(a)   an audit committee; and
(b)   a remuneration committee,
neither of which shall be regarded as a part of management.
All the members of each shall be NEDs (including the chairman, if himself a NED, otherwise the deputy chairman). There should be no fewer than three members of each such committee. Other standing committees might be desirable e.g. an environmental committee, a pensions committee, a human resources committee.

2.1.2 Each committee of the board shall provide a written report of its decisions and recommendations (rather than details of discussions) to the full board for circulation through the company secretary. Directors not on the audit or remuneration committees shall attend meetings of such committees by invitation only.

2.2   It shall be a part of the task of the members of the audit committee to satisfy themselves as to:-
● systems of internal financial control;
● the adoption of appropriate accounting principles;
● the appropriateness of adopting a going concern basis;
● compliance with accounting principles;
● liaison with the auditors as to their audit work;
● monitoring rotation of the audit partner;
● discussion with the auditors of all points of principle arising from their audit work including points raised in their management letter;
● recommending to the board a fair and appropriate level of audit fees.

The audit committee should be aware and keep under review the involvement of the audit firm in working for the company on any consultancy matters, evaluating the nature, extent and costs of other work (e.g. consultancy, taxation) carried out during the year under review by the audit firm.

The audit committee should periodically review the policy, performance, management and custodianship of the company's pension funds, unless a standing pensions committee is set up.

2.3   It shall be a major part of the task of the remuneration committee:-
●   to review the levels and bases for remuneration of the executive directors;
●   to negotiate the terms of service agreements for executive directors and their severance payments;
●   to determine the levels of participation by executive directors in share option schemes and the like;
●   to coordinate and manage (sometimes to initiate) the selection process for promotions, recruitment and retirement of directors.

The remuneration committee should also, at least every three years, commission independent reports from suitable management consultants on executive director appraisals, as to the level of executive director remuneration packages, and as to the rates of NED fees.

3.   The functioning of the board

The successful functioning of the board shall be primarily at the initiative of the chairman and company secretary. Such functioning is typically dependent upon:-
●   regularity of its meetings;
●   the circulation of requisite board papers in advance and in good time (not less than five business days should be the objective except for urgent matters);
●   firm but sympathetic control from the chair;
●   orderly but free ranging discussion;
●   efficient taking of minutes (recording conclusions reached) rather than details of the debate (but with a note of dissentient views) by the company secretary and their prompt circulation after the meeting;
●   a clear understanding of 'reserved' subjects which require board approval prior to action or implementation by the executives; a list

of such subjects shall be given to each director, and amendments sent to each director when approved.

Board papers and board agendas should include a number of standard items (e.g. financial results to date, cash flows - historical and projected, trading performance and prospects will be common to almost all companies) plus other relevant recurring items (determined by the nature of the company's activities). Additionally, over the course of each financial year, each major trading division or subsidiary should make a presentation to the board, thus involving the attendance of divisional and subsidiary managers at board meetings. The objective should be to ensure that board members have an understanding of the operation and financing of the group and opportunities to evaluate and assess the effectiveness of executive directors and those to whom management functions are delegated by the board. The board should devise and adopt a regime for the division of executive responsibilities, and such regime should be kept under review and updated as and when appropriate in the light of changing circumstances.
No one individual shall have delegated to him sole and unfettered powers of decision on any matter of a nature or exceeding an amount which shall be prescribed and adopted by the board from time to time. Such matters (the description of which will vary from company to company) shall only be proceeded with after, and subject to the terms of, board approval.

4.   The board and its accountability

4.1   Whilst financial accountability and the clarity and formal presentation of the company's interim figures and its annual report and accounts are ultimately matters for the board as a whole, the work of the audit committee should be seen to be of importance, and the board shall be made fully aware of any critical comments emanating from the committee and from the auditors themselves. Each director (whether or not on the audit committee, but particularly if so) shall be regarded by his colleagues (NEDs and executives), by the shareholders and as a matter of legal obligation as having a primary duty to draw attention publicly (e.g. in the annual report and accounts and in any resignation or retirement statement) to matters which materially fall short of proper expectations and have not been adequately reflected elsewhere (e.g. in the accounts, perhaps in the directors' accounting responsibility statement) or have not been corrected or are not being corrected and remedied.

The annual report and accounts shall contain a statement by the board as to directors' responsibility for the preparation of such report and accounts and in particular as to the adequacy and appropriateness of the company's systems of internal controls, accounting principles, adoption of a going concern basis, and compliance with the accounting principles. Such statement should be printed next to (but above) the report of the auditors.

4.2   The directors' report accompanying the annual accounts shall contain a compliance statement as to the extent to which the mandatory requirements of this Code have been adopted and adhered to, with explanations as to the extent (if any) that they have not been and reasons therefor. Such explanations should be given in sufficient detail for shareholders to understand and evaluate the reasons, and shall contain a statement of future policy as to adoption of and adherence to all such requirements.

4.3   The directors' report (or, if preferred, a note to the accounts) shall fully disclose the emoluments of each and every director (both executive and non-executive) split into their salary and (for executive directors) performance related and other (e.g. pension funding) elements. The basis on which performance is measured shall be explained in summary form.

4.4   Boards of companies with pension funds shall include in the directors' report a statement of their policy, and their attitude towards funding and the inadequacy thereof. There shall also be included a statement of the names of the trustees of the funds, by whom they are administered and by whom they are held and by whom the funds are invested. Any connection of any such persons with any director or major (3% plus) shareholder in the company shall be disclosed. The company itself shall not be a trustee. Some of the trustees should be NEDs. The administrator should not also be custodian of pension fund assets.

4.5   The board should, periodically and where appropriate (having regard to the nature of the company's business and assets) commission an environmental audit and a management audit respectively. Shareholders should be informed that it is the policy of the company to do so and to implement suggestions and recommendations made as a result of such audits as the board sees fit. The audit reports themselves should, however, be regarded as confidential to the board and to the company's advisers.

B Pro forma letter of appointment for non-executive directors

Dear

I am happy to confirm that at a board meeting held earlier today you were appointed a (non-executive) director of the company subject to the Articles of Association, an appointment you have signified to me that you were willing to accept.

We have already provided to you a wide range of financial and general information so that you could assess the implications of such an appointment.

You are aware that under the company's Articles of Association, your appointment by the board has to be put before our shareholders at our next annual general meeting, and at that meeting you must formally retire as a director but will be eligible for re-election until you come up for retirement by rotation again, typically three years later.

How our shareholders vote on this (and indeed any) issue is a matter for them. Our board policy is that our non-executives should serve for successive periods of three years, with a review at the end of each such period.

You will be requested to serve on our [audit] [remuneration] committee[s]. I have explained to you the constitution and the present composition of [those][that] committee[s], and the tasks assigned by the board to them.

Your director's fee will (at present rates) be £........ (gross) per year and this fee is designed to cover all the time and work you will be devoting to our affairs. You will not be eligible for any other benefits (e.g. bonuses, special duty payments, membership of our pension scheme, or share incentive or option plans or the like) neither will you be eligible to have a company car for your own use. We will, however, reimburse your expenses on company business, including travel expenses and, where appropriate (and after a confidential discussion with me or with the Deputy Chairman) seeking independent professional advice as to the affairs of the company.

In addition, we pay for the costs of D&O insurance cover for you in connection with your office as a director of the company and you will be required to take out and maintain your own D&O cover at an appropriate level. The policy should be issued in your name, and you will be liable for any taxation arising from the fact that the reimbursement by the company of the relative premiums may be considered to be part of your emoluments. I am required to monitor compliance by each director with such provisions, and I will, from time to time, ask you to produce to me your D&O policy and cover note.

There are many other matters which are relevant to your appointment of which you are aware. Should you wish to prepare a summary of them, please let me know.

I am delighted to welcome your appointment to our board on the above basis, and look forward to working with you to the benefit of our shareholders.

I would ask you to countersign the enclosed copy of this letter to confirm the basis of your appointment with the company as one of our (non-executive) directors on our main board. This exchange of letters will be shown to shareholders when requested, and will be open for inspection at our annual general meetings.

I also enclose for your countersignature a copy of our Code as to dealings in market securities, to which all directors and certain senior employees have to agree.

Yours sincerely

CHAIRMAN
For and on behalf of the board

C Suggested pro forma code as to dealing transactions in market securities

The Stock Exchange requires that a listed company adopts a code for dealings in its listed securities for its directors and senior employees based on principles and guidelines contained in the Stock Exchange Yellow Book ('the Model Code'). The intention behind the Model Code is that it will provide a minimum standard or code of behaviour for incorporation into a listed company's own house rules.

Accordingly the following Code of Practice ('the Code') in respect of dealings in listed securities was adopted by the board on [19].

The Code sets out the procedures to be followed in connection with dealings in the shares or other listed securities of [   ] plc ('the Company') and in certain circumstances of other companies with which the Company may be involved in negotiations ('involved companies').

Part V of the Criminal Justice Act 1993 makes 'insider dealing' a criminal offence. Such an offence exists not only when an 'insider' with 'insider information' himself deals on a regulated market or through a professional intermediary in 'price-affected securities' in relation to the information, but also if he either 'encourages another person to deal, or discloses that information to another person 'otherwise than in the proper performance of the functions of his employment, office or profession'.

Compliance with the Code will not legalize a deal if it is prohibited by law nor will it constitute a defence in criminal proceedings. In view of this, any person wishing to deal in the securities the subject of the Code should, in any event, be aware of the prohibitions contained in the Criminal Justice Act.

In particular, you should note that the statutory prohibitions against insider dealing can still apply after ceasing to be connected with the Company. Accordingly, a person subject to the Code who leaves the Company or any of its subsidiaries should consider himself still subject to the Code following any termination of employment and should not deal in the Listed Securities (as defined in 1(a) below) without first consulting the specified person until the specified person has confirmed in writing that the Code no longer applies to the person subject to the Code concerned.

1.   Dealings with which the Code applies

The Code applies to the following types of dealing:-
(a)   the sale or purchase of listed shares, debentures and loan stocks of the Company, of any subsidiary or of any involved companies ('Listed Securities');
(b)   the grant, acceptance, acquisition, disposal, exercise or discharge of options or similar rights or obligations to subscribe for or purchase or sell Listed Securities ('Options').

2.   Persons to whom the Code applies

The Code applies to dealings in which the following persons have 'an interest':-
(a)   the directors of the Company ('Directors'); and
(b)   such designated senior executives or other employees as the board shall deem appropriate and the Secretary shall notify accordingly ('Notified Party');
(together and severally 'a person subject to the Code').

3.   Dealings in which a person subject to the Code has an interest

Dealings in which a person subject to the Code has 'an interest' include:-
(a)   any dealing by him or on his behalf;
(b)   any dealing by or on behalf of any person 'connected' (within the meaning of s346 Companies Act 1985) with him and including:-
    (i)   a spouse;
    (ii)   a child under the age of eighteen (including a stepchild or illegitimate child);
    (iii)   a company with which the person subject to the Code is 'associated' (namely, in which he together with other connected persons are interested in shares representing 20% or more of the nominal share capital or which carry 20% or more of the votes);
    (iv)   a person acting in his capacity as trustee of any trust the beneficiaries of which include the person subject to the Code or his spouse or any children, or an associated company; and
    (v)   a business partner (acting in that capacity) of the person subject to the Code or of any Connected Person as described in paragraphs (i) to (iv) above; or
    (vi)   an individual having the same home; and

(c)   (if a director or any person connected with him has funds under management, whether or not on a discretionary basis) any dealing by the investment manager of such funds.

4.   Prohibited dealings and duty of confidentiality

Any dealings in which a person subject to the Code has an interest will be treated as a dealing by such person and will be subject to the prohibitions on dealing and the notification requirements set out below. However, a dealing by another person (in which a person subject to the Code has an interest) will not be treated as a dealing by the person subject to the Code and will not be prohibited by the Code if by informing that other person that he is not free to deal, the person subject to the Code would thereby breach his duty of confidentiality to the Company. This relaxation is only likely to be relevant in relation to dealings **outside** close periods and which are prohibited in the circumstances set out in paragraph 6 below.

5.   Purpose of dealing

A person subject to the Code should not **at any time** deal in Listed Securities on considerations of a short term nature.

6.   Close periods

A person subject to the Code should not deal in any Listed Securities of the Company during the periods of two months immediately preceding the announcement by the Company of its interim results or immediately preceding the preliminary announcement of the Company's annual results and on the days of such announcements ('the close periods'). A person subject to the Code should, prior to any dealing in any Listed Securities of the Company, check with the Company Secretary as to the earliest projected date for such announcements.

7.   Unpublished inside price-sensitive information

7.1   A person subject to the Code should not deal in any 'price-affected' Listed Securities at any time when he is in possession of 'insider price-sensitive information' within the ambit of Rules 7.2 and 7.3 below or further or otherwise if such information might, if, as and when publicly released, be likely to have an effect on the market price of such Listed Securities.

7.2   Information of the following kind will be regarded (irrespective of such likely effect) as inside price-sensitive information at all times until such information has been notified to the Stock Exchange:-

(a)   particulars of any acquisitions or disposals by the Company or any subsidiary which would require to be notified to the Stock Exchange because of their size or because the consideration will be satisfied in whole or part by the issue of the Company's securities;

(b)   any proposed change in the capital structure of the price-affected Listed Securities of any company (including the structure of its debt);

(c)   any decision to change the general character or nature of the business of the Company or any of its subsidiaries;

(d)   any change in the status of the Company for taxation purposes which may significantly affect the tax position of the Company or its shareholders;

(e)   any information required to be notified to the Company in respect of the acquisition or the proposed acquisition by another company or by an individual of a substantial interest in the share capital of the Company;

(f)   any information relating to interests of and dealings by Directors and persons connected with a Director in the shares of the Company;

(g)   any purchase of price-affected Listed Securities of any company of its own securities.

7.3   Listed Securities will be regarded as 'price-affected' if the inside price-sensitive information in relation to them might, if when publicly released, have an effect on their market price.

8.   Notification and clearance

A person subject to the Code should not in any event at any time deal in any Listed Securities unless the person subject to the Code has first notified [the chairman] or such other director as may be designated in writing by board resolution ('the specified person') and received confirmation in writing from the specified person that such dealing may take place. In his own case the 'specified person' is required **prior** to any dealing to have notified the full board at a board meeting or alternatively the Deputy Chairman or any other director designated by the board for the purpose and to have received confirmation in writing from him that the dealing can proceed.

9.   Reasons for refusal of clearance

Subject to Rule 10 below clearance to deal **will not** and under the Rules of the Stock Exchange **must not** be given if:-

(a)   at the time the notice of intention to deal is given under Rule 8 above there exists any matter which constitutes unpublished price-sensitive information in relation to the Company's securities (whether or not the person subject to the Code is aware of such matter) and the dealing is proposed to take place before the time when it has become reasonably probable that an announcement will be required in respect of the matter;

(b)   subject to paragraph 10 below, the proposed dealing falls within a close period;

(c)   the specified person otherwise has reason to believe the proposed dealing would be in breach of the Code.

10.   Exceptional circumstances when dealing may be permitted

10.1   A person subject to the Code who during a close period wishes to and has exceptional reasons for disposing of Listed Securities (e.g. a pressing financial commitment that cannot be satisfied by any other means) may notify the specified person and seek clearance for a disposal. If the specified person, in his absolute discretion, determines that the circumstances are exceptional, he may grant clearance provided that the **only** reason for the person subject to the Code being prohibited from dealing is because the Company is in a close period and there is no other reason why the dealing should be prohibited.

10.2   An employee may be allowed to exercise an Option granted under an employee share scheme or the like which has been approved by shareholders if the final date for the exercise of such Option falls at a time when he is prohibited from dealing under the Code and he could not reasonably have been expected to exercise the Option at an earlier time when he would have been free to do so.

11.   Record of notifications and dealings

11.1   Copies of every notification made and response given under Rule 8 shall be delivered to the Secretary who shall maintain a special and separate central record of the same and who shall confirm in writing to the person subject to the Code when such a record has been made.

11.2 The dealing should take place within the period specified in the relevant written confirmation or, if no such period is specified, within five days after receipt of the written confirmation.

11.3 The Secretary shall ensure that at each board meeting there is tabled a schedule detailing all dealings in which persons subject to the Code are interested and which have been notified since the date of the last board meeting.

11.4 The Secretary shall also maintain a special and separate schedule detailing dealings or proposed dealings in which persons subject to the Code and Connected Persons are interested which shall be brought to the attention of the board and be available to members of the board at all times.

12. Dealings by Connected Persons

It is recognised that it is not always practicable for a person subject to the Code to ensure that dealings in which he is interested (and in particular dealings by Connected Persons (including trustees of trusts of which he is a beneficiary)) are conducted in accordance with the provisions of the Code, and the remoteness of some interests may make it difficult to prevent such dealings without divulging confidential information or requiring a breach of trust to occur. However, generally, if a person subject to the Code has an influence over the decisions of Connected Persons he should ensure, so far as is within his power, that they do not deal at a time when the person subject to the Code is not free to do so. In any event a person subject to the Code should ensure that all Connected Persons are aware that he is subject to the Code and of the close periods in which they will be prohibited from dealing in the Company's listed securities. In addition Directors must ensure that all Connected Persons notify him after any dealing in Listed Securities has occurred to enable compliance with Rule 15 of the Code.

Dealings by family members and connections outside the scope of Rule 9(b) unless covered by Rule 13 below, do not fall within these Rules; but any person subject to the Code must not disclose price-sensitive information to such people.

13. Persons subject to the Code who are trustees

Where a person subject to the Code is a trustee (but not a beneficiary) of a trust holding Listed Securities he will not be treated for the purposes of the Code as interested in a dealing in such Listed Securities by the trust if the decision to deal is taken by co-trustees acting wholly independently from the person subject to the Code (i.e. following a decision taken by a majority of the remaining trustees or by a committee of which the person subject to the Code is not a member). However, a person subject to the Code should, at the very least, notify his co-trustee(s) of his connection with the Company and require his co-trustee(s), if practicable, to advise him in writing of any proposed dealing and should ensure, in any event, that all completed transactions, whenever they occur, are notified to the person subject to the Code to enable him to comply (if applicable) with Rule 15 of the Code.

14. Funds under management

If a person subject to the Code or a Connected Person holds funds under professional management then he should require the manager to advise him of any dealing in Listed Securities to ensure compliance with the notification procedures contained in Rule 15 of the Code.

15. Notification obligations of directors

In addition to the notification of a proposed dealing required under Rule 8 above, a director must notify the Company Secretary immediately after:-

(i)   any transaction which results in a change in his interest or that of his spouse or child in Listed Securities; or

(ii)   any other transaction in Listed Securities by a Connected Person; or

(iii)   the grant to or by or acceptance by him or a Connected Person of any Option and the acquisition, disposal, exercise or discharge of or any other dealing with such Option.

Such notifications are required to satisfy legal requirements under the Companies Act 1985 and continuing obligations of the Company under the Stock Exchange Yellow Book. The notification under Rule 8 above will not discharge these separate notification obligations. In addition, neither notification counts as a declaration of a director's interest in contracts as required by s317 of the Companies Act 1985 [and the Articles of Association].

16.   Single company personal equity plans ('PEPs')

A person subject to the Code may enter into a single company PEP which involves regular payments by standing order or direct debit of sums which are to be invested in securities of the Company if the following provisions are complied with:-

(a)   he does not enter into the plan or cancel or vary the terms of his participation at any time when he is not free to deal in those securities; **and**

(b)   before entering into or cancelling the plan or varying the terms of his participation, he obtains clearance under Rule 8 above.

17.   Savings schemes etc

Where a person subject to the Code proposes to enter into a scheme under which securities of his company:-

(a)   are purchased pursuant to a regular standing order or direct debit arrangement; or

(b)   are acquired by way of the reinvestment of dividends or other distributions received; or

(c)   are acquired pursuant to a standing election to receive shares in place of a cash dividend;

similar restrictions and exceptions apply as set out in Rule 16 of the Code in relation to PEPs.

18.   Guidance on other dealings

For the avoidance of doubt, the following constitute dealings for the purposes of this Code and are consequently prohibited in circumstances where dealings generally are prohibited under this Code:-

(a)   arrangements which involve a sale of Listed Securities with the intention of repurchasing an equal number of such Listed Securities soon afterwards (otherwise known as 'bed and breakfast' dealings);

(b)   dealings between directors of the Company; and

(c)   a sale of Listed Securities following the exercise of an Option (for example, under an employees' share scheme) even where the exercise of the option is permitted by paragraph 10.2 of this Code.

19. Restrictions on dealings in listed securities of other companies

19.1 A person subject to the Code:-
   (a) should not at any time deal in the listed securities of any other company (including a USM company) at any time when by virtue of the position held by him in the Company or any of its subsidiaries he is in possession of unpublished inside price-sensitive information relating to those securities;
   (b) should not deal in the listed securities of any other such company if he has reason to believe that the Company or any subsidiary is or has recently been or is about to be involved in a transaction involving any of the businesses, assets or shares of that other company without first following the notification procedure set out in Rule 8 above and obtaining confirmation that such dealing may take place.

19.2 A person subject to the Code will at all times need to be particularly careful not to disclose inside price-sensitive information to Connected Persons, co-trustees and fund managers. Subject to that, he may need to advise such persons of the names of other companies falling into the category referred to in Rule 19.1, dealings in the securities of which may as a result be restricted.

I acknowledge receipt of the above Model Code and agree that my adherence thereto shall be regarded as a fundamental term of my contract of employment/ letter of appointment with the Company so as to justify summary termination in the event of my acting in breach of any of the provisions thereof.

SIGNED
DATED

Note

This suggested pro forma code may need to be reviewed when the new Yellow Book is published in the autumn of 1993.

D Checklist for new directors (before accepting appointment)

FIRSTLY

General background information

Obtain, study and raise unanswered questions (probably, through the chairman, with the company secretary) on:-

(a)   The company's Memorandum and Articles of Association, the last years' (three years at least) annual reports and accounts, pension scheme trust deed, rules and booklets and the latest report by the scheme's actuary, the identification of the company's financial advisers, solicitors, pension scheme actuary, investment managers and fund custodians.

(b)   Service agreements of main board executive directors, details of their pension provisions and of their participation in bonus or performance-linked schemes, and in share incentive or share option schemes or the like;

(c)   The group corporate structure (this will probably be in diagrammatic form);

(d)   CVs of all main board directors;

(e)   Standard form of letters of appointment of non-executive directors.

SECONDLY
(if you are happy about the general background information)

More sensitive information

Obtain, study, and discuss (probably with the chairman plus the finance director) points arising from:-

(a)   Details of the financial facilities (e.g. overdrafts, term loans, etc) available to the group, the extent they have been called on and are or are not secured, and when they come up for review;

(b)   Current year's budgets and performance to date against budget and last year;

(c)   Composition of board committees, their terms of reference, and the extent of their authority and the authority of each executive director without main board approval, main board reserved subjects;

(d)   The last three annual letters of representation to the auditors and their last three annual letters to the board (or to the audit committee) as to their findings and recommendations arising from the audit;

(e)   Recent main board minutes (over the last six months should generally suffice as an initial request);

(f)   Copies of all supporting papers submitted to the last board meeting;

(g)   Copies of main product brochures;

(h)   Particulars (a summary will generally be sufficient) of outstanding litigation, arbitrations and other disputes (including product liability and environmental matters) of a material amount or effect on the group;

(i)   Details of directors and officers insurance cover;

(j)   Current strategic/business plan.

THIRDLY
(if you are happy about the more sensitive information)

Meetings to get to know and evaluate (on a one-to-one basis) some of the following (you will be able to decide from the information already provided whom you feel you should meet prior to accepting appointment):-

(a)   The managing director/chief executive;

(b)   The non-executive directors;

(c)   Other executive directors;

(d)   The audit partner at the company's auditors.

FOURTHLY
(if you are still happy after your meetings)

Agree terms, sign letter of appointment, join the board and start attending meetings.

Notes

1.   Although, on the face of it, this seems a formidable and daunting list:-

      (a)   most groups should have all the information readily available, if they are efficiently managed and have nothing to hide;

      (b)   "time spent in reconnaissance is seldom wasted".

2.   You should make it clear at the outset that everything you are given or told will be treated in confidence and used solely to evaluate the invitation to

join the board and then (if you agree to join) to serve as information for you as a director. If you do not join, the information should be returned.

3.   Some of the information provided to you may be unpublished and price-sensitive so as to make you an insider, even before you join the board.

E Aide memoire for compiling a schedule of matters to be reserved for the approval of the board

[Extract from 'The Company Secretary' Volume II No 4. Reproduced by consent of The Institute of Chartered Secretaries and Administrators]

Companies Act requirements

1. Approval of interim and financial statements;

2. Approval of the interim dividend and recommendation of the final dividend;

3. Approval of any significant change in accounting policies or practices;

4. Appointment or removal of company secretary;

5. Remuneration of auditors (where, as is usual, shareholders have delegated this power to the board) and recommendations for appointment or removal of auditors;

Stock Exchange

6. Approval of all circulars and listing particulars (approval of routine documents such as periodic circulars re scrip dividend procedures or exercise of conversion rights might perhaps be delegated to a committee);

7. Approval of press releases concerning matters decided by the board;

Management

8. Approval of the Group's commercial strategy and the annual operating budget;

9.   Changes relating to the Group's capital structure or its status as plc;

10.   Appointments to boards of subsidiaries

11.   Terms and conditions of directors [and senior executives];

12.   Changes to the group's management and control structure;

Board membership and board committees

13.   Board appointments and removals;

14.   Terms of reference of chairman, vice chairman, chief executive and other executive directors;

15.   Terms of reference and membership of board committees;

Cadbury recommendations

16.   Major capital projects;

17.   Material contracts of the company [or any subsidiary] in the ordinary course of business e.g. bank borrowing (above £xxx) and acquisition or disposal of fixed assets (above £xxx);

18.   Contracts of the company [or any subsidiary] not in the ordinary course of business e.g. loans and repayments (above £xxx); foreign currency transactions (above £xxx); major acquisitions or disposals (above £xxx);

19.   Major investments including the acquisition or disposal of interests of more than [5] per cent in the voting shares of any company or the making of any takeover bid;

20.   Risk management strategy;

21.   Treasury policies (including foreign exchange exposures);

Miscellaneous

22. Major changes in the rules of the company pension scheme, or changes of trustees or (when this is subject to the approval of the company) changes in the fund management arrangements;

23. Major changes in employee share schemes and the allocation of executive share options;

24. Formulation of policy regarding charitable donations;

25. Political donations;

26. Prosecution, defence or settlement of litigation (involving above £xxx or being otherwise material to the interests of the company);

27. Internal control arrangements;

28. Health and safety policy;

29. Environmental policy;

30. Directors' and officers' liability insurance.

References

Draft Report issued for public comment, Committee on The Financial Aspects of Corporate Governance

Report of the Committee on The Financial Aspects of Corporate Governance, published by Gee & Co Limited

Admission of Securities to Listing, issued by authority of The Council to The Stock Exchange*

The City Code on Takeovers and Mergers and The Rules Governing Substantial Acquisitions of Shares, issued by The Panel on Takeovers and Mergers

Statements of Standard Accounting Practice, issued by the Institute of Chartered Accountants in England and Wales

Pension Trust Principles, published by the Occupational Pensions Board, 1992

Report of the National Association of Pension Funds, 1988

Occupational Pensions Schemes (Investment of Scheme's Resources) Regulations 1992

Occupational Pensions Schemes (Disclosure of Information) Regulations 1986

Occupational Pensions Schemes (Deficiency on Winding-up, etc) Regulations 1992

Principles of Corporate Governance: Analysis and Recommendations - Proposed Final Draft, issued by the American Law Institute

The Company Secretary, Vol.II No.4, published by the Institute of Chartered Secretaries and Administrators

* Most of this book was written before September 1993, prior to publication of the new 'Admission of Securities to Listing'. Quotations from the text are from the existing edition.